STARVED FOR AFFECTION

STARVED
for
AFFECTION

DR. RANDY CARLSON

Tyndale House Publishers, Inc.
Wheaton, Illinois

DEDICATION

There is only one person in the entire world that I would dedicate a book on the topic of affection to, and it has to be my wife, Donna. As teenagers, we took a chance that our love would last, and at ages eighteen and nineteen, jumped into marriage with both feet. God has been the glue. Donna has been the encourager. I've been a happy man ever since. There is no way I could have written a book about affection if I hadn't experienced it firsthand. Donna would tell you that my affection needs have stretched her at times beyond her comfort zone, but it's been through these acts of consistent love, affection, and encouragement that our marriage has lasted more than thirty-three years. Thanks, Donna, for showing me how and why affection is so important to a healthy marriage. And by the way, I've learned that when I do the dishes without being asked, I'm speaking one of her languages of affection and love, and as the baby of the family, I play that for all it's worth.

ACKNOWLEDGMENTS

Two are better than one because they have a good return for their work. So imagine what an entire team can do. It required a team effort to make this book a reality. For instance, Jan Long Harris was the first to catch my vision for a book that could help people find lasting affection in their most intimate relationship. Jan, along with Lisa Jackson, has been immensely patient with me through missed deadlines, multiple reviews, and rewrites. Without them, this book wouldn't have happened. I owe much to Jan, Lisa, and the entire Tyndale publishing team.

I also want to extend my appreciation to one of my own ministry team, Adam Colwell, who worked hard on an early draft of the manuscript. Adam has about the best attitude I've ever seen. I hope he keeps rubbing off on me.

I can't say enough about Barbara Kois. She was charged with the task of pulling together the loose ends of this creative process in order to help make the final manuscript work. She's a fine writer and editor, and ever so patient with an easily distracted author. Thank you, Barbara, for contributing your skills to this project.

I'd also like to thank my radio listeners for contributing the grist for the mill. Each of the stories in this book was developed by taking pieces from a variety of actual stories and creating composites of what I've heard from thousands of couples over the years. In those few cases where a real story was used, we took care to change the names of those who gave permission for their story or specific details to be shared.

Finally, none of this would have been possible without the support and love of my wife. Donna spent untold hours transcribing, reading, and providing feedback for this book. She has shown me the kind of affection, for more than thirty-three years now, that keeps me coming back for more. She is the love of my life, not to mention a great cook!

FREE! Discussion guide for
Starved for Affection
available at

ChristianBookGuides.com

To contact Dr. Randy Carlson for
speaking engagements,
write him at:

Dr. Randy Carlson
PO Box 68215
Oro Valley, Arizona 85737
www.randycarlson.com

Dr. Carlson regularly provides Marriage
E-mentoring e-mail support for couples—free
of charge. To sign up to receive Dr. Carlson's
free Marriage E-mentoring e-mail, or to review
his latest teaching materials please go to
www.loveyourmarriage.com

TABLE OF CONTENTS

SECTION
ONE

Chapter 1

AN
UNTOUCHED BANQUET

"All I really want from Nathan is to *feel* loved by him! I deserve to be loved!" Julie said, trying to hold back the tears.

Her husband, Nathan, quickly responded, "I love my wife very much, it's Julie who doesn't see all the things I do for her." Julie's next words have been repeated over and over in my years of dealing with couples in marital trouble: "I see the stuff he does and I appreciate it, but I don't *feel* any love between us." Sadly, Nathan is oblivious to Julie's core needs and admits that he doesn't want to be bothered with finding out what they are and how he can meet them. Investing himself into the *feeling side* of love is too much to ask. So the wall between them grows higher.

When I witness marriages like Nathan and Julie's collapsing under the weight of reality, one of the key elements missing is always an adequate dose of affection. It's a fact: When we *feel loved* by another person, the world and its pressures are more tolerable and manageable, because we know that someone actually cares about us and is willing to go out of his or her way to help us *feel loved*.

As Nathan and Julie sat in my office for counseling, Julie described her marriage. "On a scale of one to ten, our marriage is definitely down at one. My husband is not naturally an affectionate person, and we don't have any affection in our marriage. I think of romance when I think of affection—not necessarily sexual, but touching, caring, saying I love you," she said, letting the tears flow.

Down deep Julie knows that Nathan thinks he's loving her by all of the things he does for the family, but as his wife and lover she doesn't *feel loved* by him. Nathan has fallen prey to the trap of *mistaking routine for satisfaction*, and it's draining their marriage of its vitality.

The truth is evident: Julie and Nathan's marriage is *starved for affection*.

LOOKING FOR CONNECTION

Nathan and Julie's story is not unique. Many couples today live what Henry David Thoreau described so poignantly in his book *Walden* as "lives of quiet desperation" in their marriages. God made all of us with needs (that I like to call *biblically appropriate* needs), that should be met in a *biblically appropriate* marriage, which is one where both spouses try to live as God describes in the Bible. But for many married people, these needs are not being met in their marriages.

Each day they rise from bed, hit the floor, and go about their daily lives, everything seemingly normal—yet deep inside they are longing, almost frantically, to *connect* with the one person they care for the most . . . their spouse.

I see this nearly every day in my work with couples and families. And it's a problem that doesn't seem to be going away. I've been a marriage counselor for more than twenty years, and I hear of a longing for affection over and over.

Here are just some of the statements I hear regularly from callers on my radio show, *Parent Talk OnCall*, that support this idea of quiet desperation:

- "I'm famished for love in my marriage."
- "I need to be touched by my spouse in a way that he has never touched me before."
- "We live in the same house, we're raising the same kids, we're spending the same money—but we're just not connected. I don't even feel like I know her."
- "He tries, but my spouse doesn't know how to show me the kind of affection that I need."
- "I feel so all alone in our relationship."

Perhaps one of these statements echoes the cry of your heart. There you are, with the one to whom you've dedicated the rest of your life—living in the same house, eating the same food, breathing the same air . . . and yet you're desperate to *know* that person. To have *him* know *you*.

A good marriage is like sitting hungrily at a vast and sumptuous banquet table loaded with beautifully presented, scrumptious dishes. Not only does every morsel taste delicious, but also each item was specially prepared to nourish and strengthen your body. Best of all, there is an endless supply of food in the kitchen. This table will never be bare. God designed all of your relationships—particularly your marriage—to be a banquet table containing a feast for you and your spouse to enjoy as much as you want.

But maybe your marriage is anything but bountiful, and the banquet table is going to waste, untouched. The tasty appetizer of tender words is missing. The delectable side dishes of emotional closeness and spiritual satisfaction are absent. The rich dessert of sexual passion and fulfillment are lacking. The all-important main course of intimacy and trust is gone. It's a marriage supper long forgotten, eroded away by the responsibilities of children and career and by the subversive influence of negligence and indifference.

In short, you're *starved for affection.*

People who are starved for affection have already slipped past marital boredom and mediocrity and are beginning to disappear from the relationship into themselves—or into the arms of someone else. A marriage that is starved for affection is on the brink, poised to either take an abrupt dive or slowly shrivel up and die.

If you find yourself in this frightening place, you're not alone. Today there are so many marriages that are starved for affection in this country. Based on the number of people I counsel who express this complaint, I believe we're actually in the midst of a dire famine—and this is true even among Christian couples who genuinely desire to enjoy every good gift from God.

The starved person can be either male or female. Denise told me her story during our first session.

"Greg used to make me feel special and important. Now I feel like he doesn't even care about me." She went on to explain that in the initial stages of their relationship Greg talked to her, spent time with her, and actually listened to her. Now, as Denise put it, "Greg only cares about Greg. And he only cares about me when there's something in it for him, like sex."

When they married, Denise handed her heart over to Greg for safekeeping, but he didn't care for it as he should have. It wasn't that Greg had intentionally set out to hurt Denise, but that was exactly what he ended up doing. During the eleven years of their marriage, their relationship had slowly slipped from loving to lousy. Like most unaffectionate couples, it took time for these two to experience enough pain to do something about the state of their union. By then, each had replaced affectionate feelings toward each other with something else. This is common, for when loving feelings disappear, our human nature demands that we fill up that empty spot. Any feeling is better than no feeling at all.

Greg and Denise had wholly different ways of looking at feelings, founded, in part, by their personalities. Greg, an engineer, loved numbers, logic, and predictability. Denise loved experiences, people, and change. She was something of a free spirit who enjoyed being social and active. But when Denise wanted to go out and have fun, Greg wanted to stay home. Worse, when she wanted to talk about feelings and life, he didn't.

Greg thought it was a waste of time to talk much about things that seemed, to him, unimportant—things he flippantly referred to as "that touchy-feely stuff." He went so far as to tell Denise that she should find someone else to talk to—so she took him up on his suggestion and met a guy on the Web who seemed to care. Denise felt safe with this arrangement because they only talked through e-mail and, after all, Greg had given it his approval.

The distance between Denise and Greg grew, and as it did, so did Denise's cry for affection. At first she nagged Greg, but later nagging changed to frustration, then anger, and ultimately, resignation—and an unhealthy preoccupation with her male Internet friend.

All this time, Greg was Mr. Oblivious. He thought things were just fine. He figured as long as food was on the table, a roof was over their head, and Denise slept in the bed next to him every night, things were okay. Because Greg wanted nothing to do with how Denise was truly feeling, he fell prey to the idea that this structured relationship routine translated into satisfaction for Denise, which was the furthest thing from the truth.

When Greg discovered Denise's online relationship, he was upset. "When I told her to talk to someone else about her feelings, I expected it to be a family member or a girlfriend—not some guy on the Web," Greg said. "She was an ocean of needs I could never fill." Denise, like so many others, had chosen to retreat from Greg behind a self-made artificial barrier. These walls can be made of a variety of behaviors—busyness, silence, anger, alcohol, drugs, pornography—each leaving the wounded person still hurting, but with a new set of problems to overcome, compounding an already difficult situation.

Denise was so consumed by her need to feel that she couldn't peer beyond her self-protective wall to see Greg as he really was—a man about to drown in her unfulfilled expectations for affection.

Greg and Denise loved each other to a certain level, but it wasn't enough. Without affection and an understanding of how each other *felt*, their marriage had slipped to a dangerous place. *Love* is a Biblical mandate that is foundational to a successful marriage. You choose to love someone else. It's a commitment of your will. *Affection* goes a step beyond love. Affection takes the loving relationship between a man and woman in marriage into the deeper realm of tender expressions that result in feelings of closeness, passion, and security.

EVALUATING THE SYMPTOMS

Many people I talk to show signs of being starved for affection. Some are acutely aware of just how empty their marriages have become. They're hungry, and they know it. Still others realize something is not right with their relationship, but just can't put their finger on it until I suggest they are affection starved.

What about you? Do you resonate with the symptoms of affection starvation? Is tenderness, emotional closeness, sexual passion, or a combination of those absent from your marriage?

How you answer the following questions will give you a good idea:

- Do you feel close to or distant from your spouse?
- Do you feel passionate or mechanical?
- Is your behavior toward your spouse spontaneous or routine?
- Are you emotionally full or empty?
- Do you feel loved as you were meant to be loved, or is there something missing?
- Do you feel inspired or expired by your spouse's touch?
- Do you feel adored or indifferent?
- Do you feel understood or disregarded when you talk with your spouse?

If several of your answers indicate a lack of satisfaction with the current state of your marriage relationship, you may be starved for affection. You may feel lonely, angry, and bitter about the lack of affection in your marriage. And these feelings are perfectly understandable. But what should you do if you find yourself in this condition? How can you get the emotional sustenance you need from your spouse?

If you're starved for affection, you really only have three choices:

1. Leave your spouse and find someone else.
2. Leave things as they are and struggle along.
3. Tackle the problems without attacking your spouse.

If your choice is anything but that last option, there isn't much I can offer you. But if your desire is to take on the problems and solve them, I want to assure you that *there is hope* for renewed tenderness, closeness, and passion in your marriage. You *can* return to enjoying the banquet God planned for you and your spouse.

We'll talk later about those situations where one spouse has tried absolutely everything and nothing works. There are times—whether due to mental illness, addiction, or abuse—where even the steps suggested in this book aren't effective. But for most couples, one person can make changes that will impact his marriage in significant and positive ways, changes that will end the starvation and provide needed nourishment.

That's what happened when Nathan decided to apply this principle to his marriage. Nathan said, "I was miserable, so I decided to take responsibility for my marriage. Many times my wife will withdraw and she doesn't come out until I cross the bridge or build a bridge to her. So I take it upon myself to build that bridge, watch what I say and do, and purposely try to create a good relationship. If I want more intimacy or affection, I think, *I can create this if I'm willing to put some effort into it.*

"Once I became aware of who I am in Christ and who Christ is, I knew I had to change. The Bible says, 'Husbands, love your wives just as Christ loved the church' (Ephesians 5:25, NIV). So I have become more sensitive and caring toward her. I work at building intimacy with her by the words I speak and the actions I do. I don't wait for her to come into my world—I get into hers. And the dividends are really big. She's more caring, more sexually aggressive, more open to what I would like to do. We have a very good relationship at this point, and I wouldn't trade it for anything. Today our marriage is pretty close to a ten. We have problems in our family, as all families do, but we talk about things and stand together. We didn't always do that."

In this book, we will talk about specific ways you can impact your marriage for the better, whether or not your spouse wants to embark with you on the exciting road back to the banquet. Nathan took action by himself. While it took work and perseverance, Nathan and Julie are much happier today, and Julie is no longer starved for affection.

I want to assure you that there is, indeed, hope for your marriage too. In the first half of this book, we'll talk about what an affectionate marriage looks like, the causes of affection starvation, and roadblocks to achieving the rich marriage God intended for you. In the second half we'll identify specific areas of affection starvation and give some practical solutions to help you and your spouse get the affection you need in your marriage.

Chapter 2

HOW DID
WE GET HERE?

When Denise married Greg, she had high hopes but unrealistic expectations. She imagined never-ending closeness, intimacy, and oneness with her husband. What she got instead was loneliness and a hole she was unable to fill.

"Greg and I used to be close, but somehow we've fallen out of love," Denise said. "I so deeply need to be touched by my husband, but he just doesn't get it. He used to show me affection . . . but not anymore."

Even following a passionate sexual encounter with Greg, she was left feeling hollow and hungry for something real. She put it this way: "Afterward I'd feel almost dirty and resentful. I'd feel used, knowing there was so little affection outside the bedroom."

How did Greg and Denise get to the point of affection starvation?

Most marriages don't disintegrate suddenly or without reason. Over time, layer upon layer of often unintentional carelessness causes most marital problems. Just as a lack of food will lead to physical starvation, the lack of proper care and feeding of the emotional well-being of your marriage will likely result in all sorts of troubling outcomes. Do you recognize these symptoms?

- **Frustration**—You desire affection, but you find little satisfaction.
- **Sexual issues**—Sex with your spouse leaves you empty and ungratified.
- **Wandering thoughts**—You're starting to look for love in the wrong places.
- **Emotional numbness**—Feelings for your spouse are vanishing fast or are already gone.
- **Anger**—You easily become exasperated, even infuriated, at your partner.
- **Loneliness**—Your spouse is never truly *with* you. You're married, but you feel like you might as well be single.
- **Compulsive behavior**—You often use food, drugs, or alcohol to kill your emotional pain.

Denise struggled with these symptoms of affection starvation because an important principle was at work in her marriage: People affect people. In the words of poet John Donne, "No man is an island." What we do almost always has consequences for others, but never as much as in marriage. The actions, or inaction, of one spouse dramatically affect the other person.

THE WALL OF SELF-PROTECTION

"No one will ever hurt me again." Have you or someone you know ever said those words? That's a typical reaction for a person just exiting an abusive or adulterous marriage; it's also a normal response from one who is starved for affection. We build walls in an attempt to shield ourselves from hurt by keeping others at bay. The wall is usually built slowly over time, and is often constructed under a cloud of limited self-awareness. By the time I first met Denise, her wall was about head high and only inches away from totally shutting Greg out of view.

Many years ago I stumbled across a poem that clearly describes this wall-building process. Perhaps you can relate to its message:

WALLS

Their wedding picture mocked them from the table,
these two whose minds no longer touched each other.
They lived with such a heavy barricade between them that
neither battering ram of words nor artilleries of touch could break it down.
Somewhere, between the oldest child's first tooth and the youngest
daughter's graduation, they lost each other.
Throughout the years, each slowly unraveled that tangled ball of string called self,
and as they tugged at stubborn knots each hid his searching from the other.
Sometimes she cried at night and begged the whispering darkness
to tell her who she was.
He lay beside her, snoring like a hibernating bear, unaware of her winter.
Once, after they had made love he wanted to tell her how afraid he was of dying,
but fearing to show his naked soul, he spoke instead about the beauty of her breasts.
She took a course in modern art, trying to find herself in colors splashed upon a canvas,
and complaining to other women about the men who are insensitive.
He climbed into a tomb called "the office," wrapped his mind in a shroud of paper
figures and buried himself in customers.
Slowly, the wall between them rose, cemented by the mortar of indifference.
One day, reaching out to touch each other, they found a barrier
they could not penetrate, and recoiling from the coldness of the stone,
each retreated from the stranger on the other side.
For when love dies, it is not in a moment of angry battle, nor when fiery bodies lose their
heat. It lies panting, exhausted, expiring at the bottom of a wall it could not scale.
AUTHOR UNKNOWN

No matter how high the walls we've built to keep others out, we all have a need for people, the need to *belong*. This universal human need provides a doorway through which spouses can connect or reconnect with each other, a doorway into the banquet hall and access to its richly supplied table.

GETTING AWAY FROM IT ALL

Henri Nouwen discovered the need to connect while he was in an isolated monastery. He was a Harvard professor, writer, and theologian who lived a very active and seemingly fulfilling life before he decided to escape civilization for six months and live in a monastery. Nouwen described the experience in *New Man* magazine:

> I realized I was caught in a web of strange paradoxes. While complaining about too many demands, I felt uneasy when none were made. While speaking about the burden of letter writing, an empty mailbox made me sad. While speaking nostalgically about an empty desk, I feared the day in which that would come true. In short, while desiring to be alone, I was frightened of being left alone. [1]

While he lived with the monks, Nouwen experienced what a humanist might call an "existential moment"—when he became totally aware of both his separateness from all other people and his fears of being isolated from those same people.

This existential moment is a common experience for human beings. It's the moment when you disconnect from everything else in the universe: your family, your roles, and your responsibilities. For just a moment, you stop being a wife, a father, a boss, or whatever your job is in life. You recognize that you are an individual . . . that you exist all alone in this world, that you're the only one cognizant of your thoughts, the only one aware of your beating heart.

If you've ever had one of these existential experiences, you know that it results in the sudden realization that there is no one who can fully understand you—not your spouse, your children, your coworkers or pastor—no one, except *you*. There's no one who can truly ever know your life experiences better than *you* except God, of course. Yet even he might seem miles away at that moment.

And when this becomes clear, you immediately feel alone. Vulnerable. Afraid. It can be a chilling moment, especially if you see that your life is focused on the wrong priorities.

Once we realize our aloneness and need for connection with others, we can make changes that will impact our marriage in significant ways—changes that will end the starvation and provide needed nourishment.

While that existential moment can be scary, it is also essential. When we discern our utter separateness, we also discover our deep need for other people and the *number one desire* of all mankind—to *belong*. Yet in order to belong, we need a reason to exist and someone with whom to give and receive love.

Frank's existential moment happened in the hospital. He had built a very successful business, but it came at the cost of taking care of his family and his own health. He measured success on the basis of what he had accomplished and acquired. As a result, his family suffered since they always came second to his business; ultimately, Frank's health deteriorated.

Frank nearly died during that hospital stay, and as he recovered physically, he realized that, except for the obligatory visits from coworkers and other people who needed to be there, he didn't have any friends. He realized he was disconnected from his wife, who was angry at him; disconnected from his kids, who were growing up without him; disconnected from all the things that mattered to him. He was very much alone. Frank didn't know how to love his wife, Jana, but after this crisis she was willing to take the initiative in showing him how instead of continuing to wish he knew how to do this on his own.

She committed to helping her husband figure out how to love her, despite her anger and hurt from Frank's neglect over the years. She felt justified in being distant and bitter toward her husband, and yet when she saw his brokenness after his illness, she was willing to help him understand what she needed. Jana was a "heart" person to whom emotions and closeness were important. She needed Frank to pay attention to feelings even though he was naturally a "head" person whose preference was to handle issues on an intellectual plane without much emotion. After he got out of the hospital, they spent time walking, talking, and sharing what was important to both of them.

That was ten years ago, and today Frank is a different man. He knows how to love his wife; his marriage is stronger; and his health is better. He is now able to step out of his comfort zone—move from his head to his heart—and connect with his wife. He is more aware of his humanness and his mortality, and as a result, he focuses more on his relationships than on the bottom line of his professional life.

So how do we deal with this tension of being an individual and yet needing relationships, and why is it so necessary to come to terms with our reason to exist?

We must find the answers in order to help our marriage regain the nourishment needed to recover from affection starvation.

LESSONS FROM HOLLYWOOD

I confess I don't watch many movies, but the films that seem to captivate me the most are the ones in which the main character is wrestling with his existence and attempting to make sense of himself as an individual while also recognizing his need for relationships.

In *Cast Away*, Tom Hanks portrays Federal Express systems engineer Chuck Noland, who washes up on a deserted island after surviving a plane crash. At first, his survival skills are lacking, but eventually he learns how to meet his basic needs for food, water, and shelter. With this knowledge, he can probably survive physically on the island for his natural lifetime. But what is he missing? Companionship. So he makes himself a friend out of a volleyball and names it Wilson. Chuck does more than talk to Wilson—he shares his deepest emotions, especially his painful longing for his girlfriend, Kelly. Over time, Chuck forms a relationship with this lifeless ball. He cherishes his friend. One of the most powerful scenes in the film is when Wilson floats away on the ocean waves, and Chuck puts himself in physical danger to try unsuccessfully to "save" Wilson.

Talk about an existential moment!

Then there's the movie *A Beautiful Mind* with Russell Crowe playing John Nash, the schizophrenic Nobel Prize-winning mathematician. It's a stunning love story between this troubled man and his wife, Alicia. The existential moment for Crowe's character comes when Nash must make a decision about his medication. The drug makes him a miserable zombie but allows him to be well enough to maintain his marriage. When he's off the medication, he feels much better but suffers from extreme delusions . . . and Alicia ultimately can't take it. John has to choose: either use the medication and keep his wife, or stop taking the drugs but lose the love of his life. In the end, he decides he would rather have the relationship than feel "normal" but be alone.

The movie communicates how people are willing to sacrifice just about anything to preserve a relationship with another person.

But one of my favorite movies of all time is *What About Bob?* with Bill Murray and Richard Dreyfuss. It's a hilarious film about an obsessive-compulsive, multiphobic character named Bob and his relationship with his short-tempered therapist, Dr. Leo Marvin. Bob's got serious problems. He's afraid of just about everybody and everything. When Dr. Marvin leaves for a summer getaway with his family, Bob tracks him down, convinced he can't go on without Dr. Marvin's therapy sessions. "Gimme, gimme, gimme! I need, I need, I need!" Bob cries as he unceremoniously crashes his doctor's family vacation.

Once Bob fully weasels himself into the family's life, even overtaking Dr. Leo's role as a father, it's actually the psychiatrist who ends up being treated for a mental breakdown. The most interesting thing we learn between the laughs is that all Bob needed was a relationship with a family—in this case, Dr. Marvin's family—in order to be well, because then he would no longer face life alone.

Human beings need a reason for their existence, and they search for that reason in many places. Before we can successfully relate to others—including a spouse—we must find out what that reason is.

Obviously, most people will never have to survive on a desert island or overcome a cruel mental disorder to learn what these characters did about the deepest need of life. But many look to a plethora of man-made philosophies or belief systems that offer an explanation for why we're here. Before we get into specific causes of and solutions for affection starvation, let's mention just a few of these belief systems and what they can do to your marriage.

Many hold to evolution or other theories widely accepted as scientific truth. Charles Darwin, the father of evolution, sought to order the existence of man. He came to the startling conclusion that man is an animal that evolved from lower mammals over the course of millions of years and even now is still evolving to a stronger state. This worldview permeates modern science with the idea that man's purpose is limited solely to staying on the evolutionary track toward a higher form of existence. This utilitarian view of life reinforces selfishness in marriage because the strong get their way and win, according to Darwin.

Dozens of competing "religions" vie for the heart of man. The religion of most Americans is, I believe, *materialism* and its companion, *self-actualization*. The danger of materialism is viewing life solely through the context of possessions and money, omitting or minimizing spiritual issues. You'll likely remember the lyric from Madonna's popular song from the 1980s, "I'm living in a material world, and I am a material girl!" Her tune could easily serve as an anthem for where we've come as a nation in the past century, as could the bumper sticker that says, "The one who dies with the most toys wins!" Materialism becomes an idol that takes the focus away from marriage and the family as the endless quest for "more" takes center stage. Self-actualization, while theoretically meaning to become the best I can be and do what I was created to do, usually places "me, myself, and I" in the forefront, often leading to a drive to achieve goals despite the cost in relationships and health.

These concepts are human attempts to define our existence and avoid being alone. After all, if you can attain some higher plane, or buy something to keep you happily occupied, you don't have to deal with your loneliness, right? Wrong.

THE FORGOTTEN CREATOR

The problem with these ideas and the reason they don't work in relieving that inherent feeling of aloneness, is their human origination. Man can create all the beliefs or gods he wants to help him feel better about himself, but the fact remains: Only the Creator can determine the reason for the creation and only the Creator can fulfill our longing not to be alone.

The person who created the knife did so in order to cut things. Yet at home I've been guilty of using a knife as a screwdriver. Because I didn't want to go all the way out to the garage to get the tool I needed, I've broken the tip off of a nice steak knife in an effort (a little more effort than necessary) to remove a screw. The knife can be used as a screwdriver, but that isn't what it was designed to be. When I try to do something with a knife that it's not specifically created for, the knife becomes less than perfect for the task. Flawed. Incomplete.

What were humans *designed* for? What will meet our inherent need to belong, to not be alone, and to explain our existential moments? Simply this: to have relationship with each other and, most importantly, with God.

When we leave God out of our life, we misguidedly seek other ways to belong and find purpose—often destructive ways. If I just mention the word *pornography* on my radio program, the phones ring off the hook; thousands of men use porn in a futile, mistaken effort to connect intimately with something other than their wives or God.

In another misdirected attempt to belong, young people latch onto the gang culture. They may feel that their parents don't care about them or are unable to care for them because of personal problems the parents are facing. The gang seems to care because it offers a place to belong, to contribute, to follow customs and procedures, even if those practices are harmful and illegal. Their longing to belong to something larger than themselves makes even a gang seem appealing.

Sadly, professing Christians can forget God by staying mired in the sinful habits and addictions that he has already forgiven. I feel sorry for those who get up every day wondering, *Does God still love me today?* or *Will I go to heaven when I die?* If you're someone who does this, you know how these doubts undermine your sense of purpose, your very reason to exist.

It's when you understand the truth that God still loves you—and will *always* love you—whether you fail or not, that your reason for living is stabilized and your purpose in him begins to come clear.

CURSE IT ALL

Relational dilemmas are nothing new. In the Garden of Eden, Adam and Eve had it made in the shade—quite literally. There was no sin, no separation, no in-laws, no problems. Can you imagine it? All the barriers that stand between men and women today were nonexistent back then. The world's first couple was in a perfect state of relationship with God and each other. I have to believe that in that faultless state, Eve desired sexual relations with her husband as much as he did with her, and that Adam wanted emotional affection as much as his wife did. They understood each other completely and knew each other intimately. They lived the perfect life and had a perfect relationship until Eve gave in to Satan's suggestion to eat from the tree God had forbidden and Adam followed her in doing the same.

When sin and shame entered the picture, Adam and Eve instantly experienced separation from God and from each other. Even the specific curses resulting from their sin graphically portray that disunity: "He told the Woman: 'I'll multiply your pains in childbirth; you'll give birth to your babies in pain. You'll want to please your husband, but he'll lord it over you'" (Genesis 3:16, *The Message*).

The woman would long for her husband but never really capture him. Women face life relationally, and her curse is a *relational* curse. Even the word *pain* used here speaks of both physical and mental pain in its original Hebrew language. A woman will often detect problems and feel the pain more quickly when things go wrong in a marriage.

Husbands live under a *vocational* curse, burdened by the responsibility of providing for the family, of striving to make a living. In the original Hebrew the word *toil* is translated "labor," "sorrow," and "pain." In Genesis 3:17 from *The Message* we read, "He told the Man: 'Because you listened to your wife and ate from the tree . . . the very ground is cursed because of you; getting food from the ground will be as painful as having babies is for your wife; you'll be working in pain all your life long.'"

This is the way God established life for men and women after sin entered the world. But instead of acknowledging and working through these differences, men and women find themselves constantly fighting against each other and their respective curses. This is manifested most clearly in marriage and helps explain why relationships are always so challenging and often give way to quiet desperation. Since Adam and Eve, we have all gone our own way instead of living according to God's design. In short, we have all sinned and incurred the consequences.

How do we try to alleviate the results of this relational

curse? Most people wrongly choose to selfishly focus on their own needs and desires.

Barbara Dafoe Whitehead and David Popenoe are the codirectors of The National Marriage Project, and in their 2002 report on "The State of Our Unions," they asked young men to share their attitudes about sex, dating, and marriage. According to the study, those surveyed indicated strongly that they not only wanted to marry, but expected to do so. However, they overwhelmingly said that they were looking for a specific type of person to wed: a soul mate. Their definition of a soul mate was, interestingly, self-centered: "A soul mate is a person who understands me absolutely and understands me now."

I chuckled when I first read that report. I've been married to my wife, Donna, now for thirty-three years. I fancy myself as being rather insightful when it comes to people, yet I don't totally understand Donna . . . and she doesn't totally understand me. Becoming soul mates is a process between two people that takes a lifetime to achieve. But even after years and years of trying to know your spouse well, he or she may still have traits you don't fully understand.

Waiting for this elusive soul mate, however, was not the only obstacle to marriage cited by the young men surveyed by The National Marriage Project. They provided a long list of other reasons why they saw marriage as more of an unnecessary risk than a desired commitment. Some of their conclusions might surprise you:

- They can have sex without marriage more easily than in times past.
- They can enjoy the benefits of having a wife by cohabiting rather than marrying.
- They want to avoid divorce and its financial risks.

- They want to wait until they are older to have children.
- They fear that marriage will require too many changes and compromises.
- They face very few social pressures to marry.
- They are reluctant to marry a woman who already has children.
- They want to own a house before they find a wife.
- They want to enjoy single life as long as they can.

When Donna saw this list, she added a tenth reason that I thought was very astute: "Men don't want to marry because they don't want to make a lifetime commitment."

I used to be bewildered by women who chose to move in with men before marriage, but I think I now know why they do it. Women are simply trying to connect with the man in hopes that something special will happen. Unfortunately, the survey suggests that most men who cohabitate do so primarily to enjoy "free" sex—physical intimacy without permanent commitment— and there's really no social mandate to do otherwise.

No wonder men aren't walking down the aisle! Ever since the trouble in the Garden, enmity between men and women has existed.

I once received a letter from a man who had developed a list of requirements for his future spouse. I used his entire list in the book *Unlocking the Secrets of Your Childhood Memories*[2] and want to share just a portion of it here because it depicts the narcissistic attitude many people have.

She must be understanding and gentle.
She must like to read.
She must love poetry.

She must love to sing.
She must love horses.
She must love hockey and baseball.
She must love roller skating, ice skating, and fishing.

He knew, in some detail, exactly what he wanted in a woman but failed to mention even *one thing* he had to offer. It may seem that I'm picking exclusively on the guys here, but women, too, can be just as self-seeking when it comes to their relationships. People focus on having their own needs met—by their spouse, their children, their boss, or coworkers—all in a vain attempt to get out from under that overwhelming weight of quiet desperation.

Erich Fromm said, "Love is possible only if two persons communicate with each other from the center of their existence."[3] We tend to try to communicate with each other based on external things—our beauty, our wealth, our personality—instead of going to the center of our existence, to our heart where we're hurting and fearful.

We've seen that since the Fall, men and women have built walls between them—walls made of loneliness, desperation, competition, misunderstanding, and disobedience to God. They try again and again to scale or penetrate these walls by achievement, power, and selfishness, but until we become willing to put the needs of another before our own and do marriage God's way even if it seems counterintuitive, the walls will remain strong, high, and seemingly unscalable.

All human beings need love; we need to belong. Let's now look at the importance of affection in families—the first place we ought to feel like we belong—and the long-lasting effects of each person's family of origin.

Chapter 3

AFFECTION IS A FAMILY AFFAIR

"My earliest childhood memory is sitting on the front porch of our home at the age of three," Mike said to me during our first counseling session together. "My parents were divorced and my dad was our mailman. I waited for him to come and deliver the mail just so I could visit with him for a brief time until he went to the next house and then on down the street. My whole life has grown out of that experience because I have no background or way to understand love and affection."

As a child, Mike lived with his mother after the divorce, and the only times he got to see his dad were during those few minutes a day when he waited for him at the mailbox. Mike's wife, Stephanie, came into the marriage with her own struggles. As a child, Stephanie was orphaned and adopted, and she didn't receive healthy and appropriate affection from her adoptive parents. Neither Mike nor Stephanie understood affection, and they fought about it. Stephanie struggled to communicate verbally in a loving way, and when she sounded cold, Mike become angry. Stephanie saw affection as provision for her physical, financial, and emotional needs and those of the family.

"Before I became a Christian, affection was physical—

sexual—for me," Mike said. "Even today, I sometimes feel that way out of habit. And I sought affection from other sources, even cheating on my wife, causing even more problems."

Mike credits his relationship with God for the changed man he is today. But becoming a Christian didn't magically make all their problems disappear. Mike is committed to working on the marriage to prevent his own children from experiencing divorce, as he did as a child.

Mike and Stephanie's story illustrates the importance of affection in the family and the heartbreaking results when it is lacking.

We've looked at the larger world and how it shapes our outlook on life. We've seen how the various belief systems and cultural influences present today impact our need to belong and receive affection. Now let's focus on your current family and how the family you grew up in—your family of origin—may be influencing it, as Mike's childhood family impacted his adult life.

While this book is mostly about giving and getting the affection you need in your marriage, affection goes beyond marriage to your entire family. By figuring out how your childhood memories play into the way you give and receive affection, you can make changes in your own relationships that will help not only your marriage, but also the future marriages of your children as you provide them with a solid foundation of love and affection in your home.

Part of examining childhood memories includes looking at your family of origin and how it operated in the area of affection. Was it lavishly displayed or given stingily—or not at all? Did you feel like you "belonged" in your family? Did your parents hug you and tell you that they loved you? Did they frequently compare you with a sibling? The answers to these questions will help you make your family a group of individuals where no one goes hungry for affection.

Looking back will help you figure out how you became the person you are today. As I said earlier, many walls are built because of a lack of knowing who you really are and why you feel and act as you do. We're not going into any heavy psychoanalysis here, but we will try to uncover some important keys to how you view the world.

Remember, the goal is not to analyze or "fix" your spouse; the goal is to understand *yourself*.

BACK TO THE PRESENT

In order to figure out how you got to your present affection-starved state, it is necessary to examine your past. Although some childhood memories may be difficult or painful to think about, if you find yourself starved for affection, revisiting your early years will give you insights into your current situation. It's not so much that these memories *make* you who you are today, but more that they *reveal* who you are and what hidden hurts and shame you carry around. Obviously, you cannot alter your past, but you *can* change and overcome its negative influences on your life.

Ron and Jan provide an example. I met Jan after I'd finished speaking to a group of couples on the topic of childhood memories and marriage. Ron was still in the auditorium when she approached me in the foyer and said, "The more I've thought about my earliest memories, the more I'm starting to understand my marriage problem." Then she shared her first memory with me:

"I must have been six or seven years old. I had fallen down on the back porch and hurt my knee. It was bleeding and I was in a lot of pain. When I started to cry, my father yelled from inside the house for me to stop. I tried to, but I couldn't. Suddenly, I got scared that he was going to get mad and punish me. So I got up, went into the bathroom, and tried to put a bandage on my knee by myself, but I didn't know how. I got frustrated and my crying got louder. The more I wept, the more my father yelled. What I remember most is my father's yelling, and that I felt both stupid and afraid for not being able to stop crying."

Because of the impact of that memory, Jan had developed a fear of rejection, worrying that if others, including her husband, knew her as a "real" person, they wouldn't like her. Jan had become a world-class pleaser, putting her own needs behind everyone else's desires, even to the detriment of her own physical and emotional well-being.

When Ron joined us, his childhood memories revealed a completely different situation:

"Every evening after dinner, we'd get cleaned up and ready for bed. My home was a lot like a sanctuary, kind of a safe haven for me and my brothers and sisters. Anyway, the thing I remember most is that my mother would come into our rooms and rub our backs at night before we went to sleep. I really felt close to her then, and still do today."

Ron brought into his adult life a deep need for love, acceptance, and warmth. He desired and expected to receive lots of affection from Jan, but fear always held her back from showing affection. Her fears became bigger than reality, and she believed Ron was being unfaithful. While it was true that Ron wasn't happy in his marriage, he never showed any leanings toward adultery. Ultimately, this made Ron quite resentful. While he could see Jan was trying to be affectionate toward him, he could also tell that it was a chore for her. The more resentful he felt, the more rejected Jan became. They were trapped in this vicious cycle for years.

I'm glad to tell you their story has a happy ending. With counseling and prayer, Jan has made peace with her past and realizes she can be full of faith, not fear, about what God is doing in her life and marriage. Ron has experienced the difference in her and the freedom this realization has brought to their relationship. They have made a new commitment to make their relationship one characterized by affection and love.

YOUR OWN PERSONAL STORY

When Jan and Ron looked at their childhood memories, they were able to start uncovering the issues that kept them apart. I'd like you to identify one or two childhood memories as you read this book. If you already have a memory rattling around in your mind, write it down. If you still need more time to lock in on a memory, I recommend you keep reading and pause to write down your memory when it comes.

In identifying your childhood memory, make sure it's your memory *alone*, without influences from stories you've heard or photos you've seen. Second, the *farther back* you can travel into the past, the better, but don't get stuck trying to decide which one is the earliest. It doesn't matter.

Generally, I have found that a person's childhood memories go back to somewhere between ages three and nine. If you have trouble coming up with a memory, don't worry. It will come eventually. I do caution those with emotionally difficult or painful childhood memories to avoid exploring any memory that involves areas of abuse without the assistance of professional help.

Once you identify an early memory, ask yourself what *emo-*

tion this memory evokes. It's vital that you settle on a specific, emotional response because childhood memories help you experience *present-day* emotion elicited by a *past* occurrence. The memory helps create an accurate picture of who you are today.

The next step is to title your memory based on the emotional response it evoked. Below are some titles I've seen over the years. Create one that clearly describes your story:

- Bob, Mr. Perfect
- Heather, alone in a big world
- Vickie, I'm sorry to be of trouble
- Frank, get out of my way
- Nick, I did it my way
- Susan, a warm and fuzzy friend
- Amanda, the little girl afraid to fail

Ask yourself what your title tells you about the way you think and the way you respond to others, especially your spouse. What negative aspects of this statement about yourself would you like to change or even erase?

YOU CAN CHANGE YOUR MIND

God has given his children the power to change their minds, so you don't have to stay stuck in patterns from the past. One of my most cherished Bible verses is Philippians 4:8, here quoted from *The Message*: "Summing it all up, friends, I'd say you'll do best by filling your minds and meditating on things true, noble, reputable, authentic, compelling, gracious—the best, not the worst; the beautiful, not the ugly; things to praise, not things to curse."

You *do* become what you think about, and it will take more than a pep talk to get you on the right track. In order to be free from your past and move forward in the present, you need to do three things in relation to childhood memories:

- **Understand the meaning of your childhood memories as they affect your life today.** It may require a counselor to help you think this through, but this first step is vital. Pinpoint specific messages you heard often as a child and spend time figuring out how those messages affect you today. Ask yourself how the view your parents seemed to have of you shaped the view you have of yourself today. Not only will this help you understand your marriage, it will also help reveal the type of parent you are. If your childhood memories and emotions are about fear, criticism, or rejection, you may have unintentionally become critical or withdrawn as a response.
- **Challenge the lies from your memories.** A good place to start is at the beginning, with a growing faith in the One who created you in the first place. Who better can understand what you are going through and what you need than God? If you were told that you were stupid or lazy or shy, take another look at those words and ask yourself if they are true about you. Have you lived believing they were true? Refashion messages for yourself that reflect who you *really* are: intelligent, hardworking, friendly, etc.
- **Commit to change.** This is the most difficult step. Ruts grow deep over the years, and getting out of them isn't easy . . . but it's necessary. A mentor, counselor, or pastor could be a big help to you at this point. Once

you've identified false messages and committed to re-creating them to reflect the person you really are and want to be, you will be on your way to a new life of confidence, self-respect, and reliance on the God who made you just right.

Now that you have identified a childhood memory that has impacted your adult life and thought about areas you'd like to change, you are on the road to gaining an understanding of your motivations and attitudes. Once you do this exercise by yourself, talk to your spouse about his or her childhood memories so you can identify areas each of you struggles with in your marriage.

One final caution: As you and your partner discover and work through your childhood memories and their impact on your relationship, don't use the insights you gain *against* your spouse or as a tool to justify or excuse behavior. Rather, listen carefully and tell your spouse you appreciate his or her openness. You might want to take a "Memory Weekend" where you get away for a couple of days and think about the homes you grew up in and how memories from your childhood reveal who you are today. It's not a gripe session about your parents and all they did wrong; it's an opportunity for clarity and insight as you look back. Please don't correct, challenge, or analyze your spouse when he is sharing. Just listen and learn—and watch the healing begin.

A FAMILY AFFAIR

Before we get into specifics of helping your marriage get the affection it needs in the remaining chapters of this book, I'd like to stress the importance of affection in the entire family—with your children, your siblings, and the rest of your extended family. Affection should not be limited to spouses. Now that you have looked at your childhood and possibly identified areas where affection was lacking, let's talk about making your family one that is affectionate, which is really an extension of a healthy and affectionate marriage.

Remember that affection is a step *beyond* love. You may have known that your parents loved you, but they didn't display affection. Affection takes the loving relationship into the deeper realm of tender expressions that result in feelings of closeness and security. Even if this is not a description of your family of origin, you can make it a description of your family today, starting with your spouse and spreading to your children so that when they look back on their childhoods, they will be able to say, "We had an affectionate family."

A basic need

From birth, every human being has a need to be touched, held, and cared for. When our three children were babies, we spent hours holding, rocking, cuddling, kissing, and playing with each of them. They brought us great joy—most of the time. We enjoyed being affectionate with our children but we also realized that being touched and cared for was an essential ingredient in their development. Extensive research has shown that a child who is untouched, unloved, and uncared for usually ends up with psychological scars and lacks the ability to bond and relate well with other people.

This need is so widely recognized that volunteers all over this country visit hospitals to hold and cuddle babies who have been abandoned so they can have a better chance at normal development.

I believe God has wired us so that from the very beginning,

we need that feeling of affection, love, and security as well as food, water, and protection. And while the need for food, water, and protection never goes away, we sometimes think the need for affection does. But it doesn't. It may be masked by other more apparent needs, but at the core of every human being, no matter what age, is the basic need for affection, first from his or her family.

The family is designed by God to be the place where all of our basic needs and training for life will be provided. That's why the early years of life are so important for a child. The way a parent chooses to love that child marks his or her life forever.

Dads and daughters

Dads do four things for their daughters:

1. We set them up for success or failure in adult relationships. A girl's first and most important view of men comes from her father. A father who is lovingly supportive, affectionate, and encouraging is likely to raise a confident daughter who will choose the right kind of man if she chooses to marry. When a father is critical, abusive, distant, or absent, his daughter is more likely to go through life looking for affection in all the wrong places.

I probably fell short in raising my own daughter, Andrea. I was busy and didn't always understand her needs. If I could rewind the clock and relive those early years with my daughter, I would do two things better. I'd be better at listening to her needs and interests in life even though, as a man, I didn't understand half of them. And I would spend more time showing her physical affection.

2. We give them a picture of God. Many women struggle with their view of God because of the negative qualities they've seen in their fathers. Women with loving, supportive, and affectionate fathers are better able to accept God as a loving, supportive, and affectionate heavenly Father. Fathers are often "God with skin on" for their girls.

3. Dads help keep their daughters from seeking unhealthy affection from other men. Many tears have been shed by women who, in a desperate search for the love and affection they never received from their fathers, went to all the wrong places and people to fill that need. Some have experienced multiple marriages, abuse, and other types of self-destructive behaviors, all in a search for the kind of love and affection they should have received from their fathers.

4. Dads help their daughters develop healthy self-esteem. Wise dads never joke about their daughter's developing body because they know that undermines a girl's confidence at a time when confidence is hard to come by. Dads need to honor their daughters and show them the appropriate affection they need. By participating in a daughter's academic, athletic, and artistic activities and affirming her abilities and successes, dads build the self-esteem and self-confidence that are so necessary to becoming a healthy woman with normal needs for affection from others.

Mothers and sons
Mothers set the stage for their sons' future relationships as well.

1. Mothers represent women to their sons and influence the choices they make concerning women. If Mom is warm and supportive, a son will feel comfortable and at ease with this kind of woman because that's what he's used to. If Mom is harsh and cold, her son could gravitate toward this kind of woman. If Mom is comfortable with herself and has an appropriate level of self-respect, her son will be more likely to respect other women. But if she's a doormat who allows herself to be mistreated, he will think that's the way women are to be treated.

2. Mothers provide invaluable teaching and training to their sons. While the father-son relationship is obviously very important, Mom shouldn't leave discipline and instruction up to Dad. She needs to show affection to her son, but she also needs to be firm and not permit him to ignore her or expect her to wait on him. She must hold him accountable, even for simple chores like doing his own laundry when he's old enough and cleaning up after himself.

3. Mothers help build healthy self-esteem in their sons. As a boy sees his mother showing respect and love to his father, he comes to believe that men are worthy of respect. If she treats his dad with contempt or engages in male-bashing, her son will think men are simply an object of ridicule to women and others.

4. Mothers help instill faith in their sons. Many men credit their mothers with reading the Bible to them as children and praying with and for them. By demonstrating reliance on God in both good times and bad, mothers provide an example of turning to God in all situations.

Of course, fathers have an enormous responsibility and opportunity to influence their sons for good and show them how men who love and obey God behave, and mothers have a similar role with their daughters.

DOING IT MY WAY

It's perfectly normal and healthy for children to want increasing independence as they grow older. Most parents understand this and desire independence at the appropriate time for their children as well. Reaching independence can be a bumpy ride for both parent and child, especially during the teen years. Many parents remember the first time their child started to push them away, especially in front of their peers. They may have wanted a parent driving them to school to drop them off a block away or refrain from good-bye hugs and kisses in front of their friends.

Some parents pull away from their children during this period, erroneously believing they don't need affection any longer. I'd suggest, instead, a change in strategy. When your child begins to seek independence, it's more important than ever for her to know you love her and still want to express affection to her. Although you want to respect her desires not to hug and kiss her in public (or even in private if that's her desire), don't stop touching her or expressing affection verbally. A pat on the arm, a hand on a shoulder, a brief hug or kiss or whatever other form of expression is comfortable for you and your child, along with saying, "I love you," "I'm proud of you," and other affectionate statements will always be appropriate and helpful for your teen.

Without appropriate affection, teens may turn to destructive behaviors in an attempt to feel loved, as when teenage girls fall into the arms of the wrong guy in their desire to find affection and that all-important sense of belonging. While we as parents need to offer increasing independence to our children as they show responsibility and readiness, we also need to maintain our loving authority and demonstrations of affection at the same time.

MAKING YOUR OWN MEMORIES

Earlier we showed how childhood memories helped shape you into the person you are today. Even though you can't step back in time and change things for yourself, you have an exciting opportunity—no matter what age your kids are—to make some good memories with them. If you've made mistakes in the past and have not been affectionate with your children, it's not too late to start now. They may be surprised, but I can promise you it will be a pleasant surprise. Even if your children are now adults, reach out to them—engage them—and start some new activities that can become traditions and make good memories between you and your children and grandchildren, if you have them. Adults need affection and approval from their parents too.

Our three children are all grown now, but whenever we're together I try to hug them and show affection freely. My role as the father of adult children has changed in the area of authority, but not in the area of love.

It's never too late to begin showing affection in your family. Deep rifts have been healed by a parent of any age reaching out to an adult child, breaking patterns of decades, by showing affection and appreciation. Healing can occur at any age. And so can hurt.

Tom went into his family's accounting business in order to please his father. He wouldn't have admitted it, but deep down he knew that to get his father's attention and love, he had to follow in his footsteps. After he joined the business Tom realized he hated accounting, but he hoped that staying in the job could bridge the gap in his relationship with his father. Instead, Tom's father criticized him and the way he did his job. Tom had always wanted to be close to his father, but his father was a person who could never be pleased. None of Tom's efforts could secure his father's approval. In Proverbs 13:12 we read, "Hope deferred makes the heart sick" (NLT). Tom experienced the meaning of this verse because he did a job he hated for the man he loved, without receiving the acceptance he needed and hoped for.

THROUGH DIFFERENT EYES

A parent can have three children, all of whom grow up in the same family with the same parents in the same home, and yet each child may have vastly different memories of their childhoods. Why? Because our memories are personal perceptions based on our view of life. Of the millions of things that happen to us when we are children, we selectively choose those memories that are consistent with the way we view life today. For example, two brothers may be very different: one is outgoing, positive, and successful and the other is bitter, angry, unsuccessful in relationships, and seems to jump from job to job. Each will project onto his childhood memories the person he is as an adult. Both were raised in the same environment by the same parents and received about the same amount of attention or lack of it. But each chose different paths; the path each chose makes a difference in the memories they bring into adulthood.

The outgoing brother may remember the fun times he and his brother had playing softball with their dad, while the bitter brother remembers the time he was sick and Dad took his brother out to play in the park anyway, reinforcing the bitter fellow's misconception that his sibling was Dad's favorite. Of course, there are times when siblings remember childhood differently because they have indeed been treated differently. The favorite is cherished and adored while the unwanted child is scorned and ignored. Such horrible injustices do happen.

But each of us chooses, at some level of consciousness, how we will interpret and remember our memories. This is a very important point for a parent to recognize. Since each child is different, each needs to be parented differently. The only way you can know your child is to get behind his or her eyes and try to see life the way he or she does so you can understand what kind of memories are being built. In fact, by the time a child is ten years of age, you can ask him or her about earlier memories and you'll start to see some themes as to how this child views life.

I talked to a woman named Shirley who had vivid memories of heavy doses of criticism and rejection, particularly from her father. Their home was well cared for, she had the best of everything, and she went to the finest private school in her community. As the oldest of two, she felt pressure to be perfect. When I asked her to share a childhood memory, she immediately went back to about age eight or nine when she started taking piano lessons. After practicing for weeks, she was proud of how much she had learned and was excited to perform. But during her recital, she lost her place in her Thompson piano book and was disappointed in her performance. What she remembers most vividly are the words and disapproving look of her father who said, "You didn't listen. I told you you needed to practice more." As she described the memory, her face fell, the tears came, and I saw the devastating result of this memory on her life. Today she is hypervigilant, watching for criticism, becoming defensive to the point of anger when faced with criticism, even if it could be helpful. She's fearful of trying new things, has difficulty in genuine giving and receiving of affection, and lives a rather guarded life in her relationships.

While it's unfortunate that her dad made the discouraging

statement to Shirley when she already felt bad about her recital performance, we can't conclude that his one statement made her oversensitive and fearful as an adult. Over the years she began to interpret looks, words, statements, and criticism in a consistently negative way. Instead of being able to handle them correctly by taking the good from such statements and letting the rest go, negative statements became a part of her personal perception of life. She remembers that particular memory because it's consistent with who she is today. Each of us has a personal worldview or perspective on life, and many factors contribute to that view, including our home life, our personality, and our temperament. As adults we tend to choose to remember the childhood memories that are consistent with the way we view life. Certainly a critical father or mother impacts the children, but we must put our memories into context and tell ourselves the truth about the memory and how significant it really was. Shirley's father was a loving dad, yet she chose at some level to remember a particular critical remark he made to her. Our memories don't *make* us who we are, but they *reveal* who we are.

Another woman named Heather grew up in a home like Shirley's with everything she needed for comfortable living, but she recalls warm, affectionate, and loving memories of her father. She recalls, for example, the time when her father was helping her learn to ride a bicycle and she was afraid she would fall off. He ran along behind her, holding the seat and reassuring her that he would be with her and keep her safe. There may well have been times when Heather's father also said she hadn't practiced the piano enough, but Heather's personality or disposition led her to hold on to the good memories and focus on them. These memories are consistent with the way Heather has grown up, and, unlike Shirley, she's a trusting, outgoing woman who is able to openly express affection within her family.

An exercise you might want to do with your children is to have each family member over the age of ten write specific events he or she remembers from the past and the emotions associated with them. Make it a family affair by talking about what each person remembers from earlier years, what the memory means, and how it impacts views of life today. Not only can you as a parent learn more about your child's perceptions and personality, you can learn key areas in your parenting that you must focus on in order to provide healthy, positive memories for your child.

While we each are born with a personality, traits, and abilities unique to ourselves, all of us can change our attitudes and perceptions. God does, after all, promise to renew us inwardly day by day (2 Corinthians 4:16). We can change the way we look at things and the way we respond to them.

PRACTICE MAKES PERFECT

If you're practicing the wrong thing—like criticism or anger—your family will become accomplished in all the wrong things. It takes ten positive, affirming comments to overcome every negative comment. Consider what you are "practicing" in your family, because it is becoming ingrained as you do it over and over.

Start by taking this family assessment.

Circle one word from either column 1 or column 2 that most accurately describes the overall family atmosphere you grew up in. Then circle one word from either column 3 or column 4 that best describes the overall family atmosphere in your family today. Don't think too long because that can cloud your feelings.

FAMILY OF ORIGIN		YOUR FAMILY TODAY	
1	2	3	4
Supportive	Aloof	Supportive	Aloof
Encouraging	Discouraging	Encouraging	Discouraging
Warm	Cold	Warm	Cold
Close	Distant	Close	Distant
Real	Phony	Real	Phony
Helpful	Critical	Helpful	Critical
Open	Closed	Open	Closed
Unified	Divided	Unified	Divided
Affectionate	Unaffectionate	Affectionate	Unaffectionate

Most families fall somewhere in the middle. The words you circled represent your perception only. It shouldn't surprise you if your siblings, your spouse, or your children were to take this quiz and their answers were different, because they are different people with their own perceptions.

Now compare the words you circled under "Family of Origin" with those you circled under "Your Family Today."

- 🎴 Do any patterns emerge?
- 🎴 What do you like about your family today?
- 🎴 What would you like to be different in your family today?
- 🎴 What can you do to make things different today?

This exercise can help reveal the type of family atmosphere you have today. If your family atmosphere is one of heavy criticism, it's likely that either you or your spouse or both of you have childhood memories of criticism that you have brought into your family today. If your family atmosphere is loving, supportive, and encouraging, it's likely that one or both of you have childhood memories indicating love and support. We carry our family atmosphere from generation to generation. As the Bible says in Numbers 14:18, the sins of the fathers are passed on to the children of the third and fourth generations. This doesn't mean that God punishes the children for what their fathers do, but that often the very sins that exist in one generation also exist in subsequent ones. The wonderful news is that we can break the cycle if we choose to.

TAKING THE PULSE

How brave are you? If you dare to do it, your children are old enough to understand, and you are mature enough to handle their answers, try talking about their perceptions of what it's like in your family. You may be pleasantly encouraged or you may be well warned about problems. Copy the columns on page 47 and give one to each family member to complete independently. Then discuss it as a family, using topics like these to get each person's input:

1. Share a time when you felt loved.
2. Share a time when you felt unloved.
3. How could we make our home and family a more loving place?
4. Describe three things you like about our family.

This discussion could be encouraging or hurtful, but either way it will provide a baseline for understanding where you are today and what you need to do to become a more affectionate and loving family.

WHICH PATH FOR YOU?

Robert Frost's often quoted poem, "The Road Not Taken," reminds us that the path we choose in life will make all the difference. We can either take the road of affection with our spouse, our children, and our extended family, or we can choose to hold back. What do we have to lose by taking the road less traveled, the road of warm, open affection? The only thing we'll lose is the pain we experience when there is distance in these important relationships.

Chapter 4

WHAT WE DO
FOR LOVE

When you're really hungry, almost anything will do. When we were visiting Israel, the guide took our tour group to a small, out-of-the-way village with an assortment of interesting people and quaint shops loaded with unusual trinkets. Most intriguing, however, was the food, much of which hung from dirty meat hooks in the storefront display, apparently to entice people like us and a variety of native bugs. Suddenly, the thought of authentic village dining didn't seem that appealing, especially for Donna, whose idea of sanitary ranks right up there with that of Mr. Clean.

But after a few more hours of walking and shopping, lunch-time rolled around and we found ourselves in the same little town with the storefront displays of bug-infested meat. For Donna and me, the traditional before-meal prayer took on a whole new importance. I must confess we both kept our eyes closed as we began to consume the culinary delight we were served. We didn't really want to see what our lunch looked like, much less guess what it was called—or how long ago it had been alive. Hunger drove both of us to eat first and ask questions later.

Here at home, things really aren't a whole lot different. The fast-food industry thrives on convenience, rather than on quality. Some restaurants could hardly exist if Americans took nutrition seriously. But when you're really hungry, you're driven much more by need than discernment.

When you're affection hungry, you'll settle for just about anything, too.

Your need for belonging, closeness, and someone to care for can cause you to do, well, some pretty stupid things that'll quickly mess up your life and marriage. These things are just like some fast food: strong on convenience, but short on quality.

ALL THE WRONG PLACES

In my first conversation with Jacob, his desperation was clear: "If something doesn't change in my marriage pretty soon, I'm just going to get out!"

He was deeply discouraged because he and his wife, Gail, had been fighting for years. No matter what the issue, things generally ended with both spending several days pouting and hiding out from each other. Eventually they would reconnect in some fashion, but this endless cycle of petulance and withdrawal was taking a deadly toll on their relationship, especially for Jacob. He said they had both tried counseling, but it hadn't worked, which told me neither person was quite ready to take responsibility for the marriage mess. As I probed deeper, I began to see why.

Jacob revealed that he and Gail had gotten married only after discovering that she was three months pregnant. They had lived together for the previous two years, an arrangement Jacob said was born more out of convenience than love. Yet both wanted to do the "right thing" for the sake of their unborn child, so they wed more out of obligation than commitment. Love and affection were pencil thin.

Jacob and Gail both wanted to experience closeness, but

neither was receiving it from the other. Moreover, Jacob admitted that neither of them had been, or were now, deeply in love with the other. He said he knew Gail resented having to get married, leaving him feeling trapped. In his frustration, he confessed that he was increasingly turning to pornography in an attempt to fulfill his need for affection. Ultimately, this led Jacob to an impulsive one-night stand and a sexually transmitted disease.

You see, Jacob needed love, but he looked for it in the wrong places. He did something incredibly stupid and was paying the price. If you're starved for affection, you too are extremely vulnerable and could be on the verge of doing something stupid like having an affair or falling into an addiction. Perhaps you already have. We will talk later about the need for repentance and forgiveness, even when you feel like throwing in the towel.

Take a look at the following questions. Be completely honest as you consider your answers, which will indicate your level of vulnerability:

- When you see other couples expressing affection, do you wish your relationship were more like theirs?
- Do you regularly fantasize emotionally or sexually about another person?
- Is it getting more difficult for you to please your spouse?
- Do you ever think about divorce?
- Do you criticize your spouse to your friends or family?
- Are there secrets you keep from your spouse?
- Do you go out of your way to completely avoid conflict with your spouse?
- Have you ever wished you had never gotten married?
- Do you ever think that you'd be happier with someone else?

■ If you could marry your husband or wife again, do you wonder if you would?

If you answer yes to several of these questions, it's time to take some action. While most people have probably had fleeting angry moments when they wished they hadn't married their spouse, if you persistently think this way, you're likely unguarded and weak enough emotionally to make a mistake that could have painful and even tragic consequences for your relationship.

Are you curious as to how your spouse might answer these questions? Ask him or her—but only if you're ready to face the possibility that you're going to have to do some hard work to make your relationship better. The answers to these questions may lead you and your partner into areas where you need a counselor to help you work through the issues. I also recommend marriage workshops, books, and tape series by reputable Christian counselors, authors, and teachers. But regardless of where you find yourself or your marriage, you can work through your problems with effort and commitment. It's possible—couples are doing it every day.

Now let's look at some of the wrong places married people look for affection: in manipulative emotional games we play with our spouse; in fantasies; in addictions to work, gambling, drugs, alcohol, or other substances; or in opposite-sex friendships.

STUPID THINGS PEOPLE DO

Starvation usually brings out the baser characteristics of humanity. It breaks my heart to see footage of starving people in other parts of the world fighting for a bowl of grain. These people live where either food supplies are restricted or food production is low. Poverty, war, and illness also combine to rob babies of basic sustenance. When precious supplies of food reach these people, offering them at least temporary hope, they quickly eat whatever they get with thanksgiving to God. They know what it's like to be truly needy, and they appreciate what they receive. Here in the United States, we often take for granted the food, advanced medicine, and freedom we have.

It's also sad to watch people waste away from affection starvation when there's plenty to go around. The banquet table is full. Yet far too many marriages try to survive on a diet of scraps from the table of love. It's an unnecessary reality. Except in the cases of mental illness and some extreme physical disabilities, God has equipped each of us to give and receive affection in our marriage. The excuse of "I'm just not an affectionate person" doesn't hold water. We've been commanded to love one another, which includes acts of love and touches of affection. When we don't honor this command we place ourselves and our spouse in a precarious place. Understandably, we begin to look for release and comfort when we're hurting. But seeking that solace in the wrong places will only lead to more pain. Some of the inappropriate ways people try to feed their starving marriages include:

- threatening divorce
- withholding love
- playing sexual games
- having an affair
- diving into pornography or other harmful addictions

Jacob and Gail were both doing some pretty stupid things in their quest for love. While he gave in to porn, Gail turned to food. Both were diversionary strategies to avoid dealing with the underlying issue between them. Neither strategy worked. But Jacob took the lead in coming to me for help with his marriage. He didn't wait for Gail to take action or begin to change. He took responsibility for the situation and acted in a positive direction.

TAKING WHATEVER YOU CAN GET

I began counseling individually with Jacob and Gail. When I asked Gail what originally attracted her to Jacob, her answer showed a lack of depth in her feelings toward him. "I really liked Jacob's smile," she said, "and he treated me nice." Enough for a first date, perhaps, but certainly not enough to form the foundation of a lifetime commitment. When I asked Gail why she married him, she said, "Well, I thought we could make it work. And, of course, I felt the pressure of being pregnant and I wanted my baby to have a father. So we did what seemed right at the time."

It was easy to see that Gail's attraction to Jacob was a bit thin and that the strength of commitment was questionable. Jacob's responses were similar. "I felt trapped. I wanted to finish college and get a good job before getting married to anyone. When Gail got pregnant, I felt obligated to marry her and try to make it work."

Jacob and Gail made the tough decision to put their child's needs above their own and make their relationship work, but unfortunately, both of these attractive young adults felt they were settling for second best.

Over the weeks that followed, I helped Jacob and Gail to make an important decision, one that would later prove to be the pivotal moment in their relationship. They made the decision to *start over* with each other.

Jacob started by admitting his porn problem and agreeing to see a specialized counselor for help. At first he did this only for his own benefit, but he soon discovered it would have an incredibly positive impact on his marriage. Jacob learned he had been settling for an illusion of intimacy, and that the real stuff—the *good* stuff—was only a heartbeat away, inside of Gail, waiting to be poured out to him.

Gail confessed to Jacob about how she felt pressured to get married, but that she really did want their relationship to survive. She also committed to stop letting food be her comfort and begin eating healthier foods.

Both Jacob and Gail began to understand that, instead of providing nourishment to each other, they had chosen to get by on whatever affection scraps they could find. Jacob had turned to the empty promises of porn. Gail turned to food for comfort. Both approaches left them empty. Some other popular watering holes for the affection-starved person include:

- workaholism
- alcohol and drugs
- gambling addictions
- affairs
- entertainment

If you're desperate enough for affection, you may even be tempted to go *too far* in trying to get it from your spouse. Groveling, begging, or demanding will not work. These adolescent approaches to love always fail, because in the process of trying to get what you need, you'll raise a wall of disrespect that will not be easy to break down. In fact, what attracts a person worth keeping is self-respect and confidence. Your spouse values herself as a child of God created in his image and she knows she is capable of doing the work he created her to do. If a spouse is overly needy for love and affection in marriage, he or she might avoid confrontation, turning a blind eye to destructive behavior on the part of a spouse, and as a result, actually help the person continue in the harmful behavior.

CHASING FANTASIES

I've seen both winners and losers in the game of marriage. What I've discovered is that those who successfully weather the storms of marital challenges reverberate with one theme: They hang in there for the long haul and learn to truly love and demonstrate affection to their spouses.

Jacob's and Gail's expectations were rooted in unreality. They had "played house" for two years, living like a married couple but without the commitment of a married couple. If you're living in a dreamworld relationship, do yourself a favor and get your feet back on the ground. I'm not asking you to deny that your spouse is unaffectionate and unloving, but I am imploring you to resist the false lure of fantasies with hollow promises.

It's not sheer fantasy to have a dream for your marriage. You *need* a dream for your relationship. In fact, I've dedicated an entire chapter to helping you and your spouse develop "vision intimacy" centered on goals for the future. Through establishing a vision as a couple you can experience incredible affection as you pray, plan, and work together to turn your dreams into reality.

But unrealistic dreams are just illusions. Hollywood portrays a kind of dreamworld that simply doesn't exist. Movies and television present passionate sex and romance and round-the-clock affection as the ideal, even the norm. If your love life falls short, there must be something terribly wrong with you. That simply isn't true. In the real world, clothes need to be washed, cars need to be repaired, grass needs to be cut, snow needs to be shoveled, bills need to be paid, and children need teaching and discipline. These life demands take a high toll on the time for creating romance and showing affection in marriage.

One woman I talked to admitted openly that she frequently thought about a man she dated back in college twenty years earlier. Over time, these images of her happy college years had taken on larger-than-life proportions. It became impossible for her forty-five-year-old, slightly overweight, balding husband to ever measure up to the image of the athletic, dark, and handsome twenty-two-year-old college guy she once dated. She privately compared what she had in reality with what she thought she should have in her fantasy. She somehow figured she deserved more. The image of this young man (who now might well be forty-five, slightly overweight, and balding, too) was frozen in her mind.

Unrealistic thinking does three destructive things to marriage:

1. Focuses on things you can't have, which is *coveting*
2. Takes your mind off what you *do* have, which is *ingratitude*
3. Creates unreasonable expectations, which lead to *disappointment*

I was once pulled over by the state police for a burned-out taillight on my car. It turned out that he regularly listened to my radio program and, after giving me a written warning, he asked if we could talk. I got out of my car and together we moved out of the way of the busy highway traffic.

With his car's flashing lights still warning the oncoming traffic to slow down and gawk at the latest traffic criminal, this police officer described a marital disaster. His wife was involved in another kind of dreamworld, the world of fantasy. "I've lost my wife to the fantasies of daytime television," he said. "She's completely taken with those ridiculous stories. She is constantly reading romance novels and articles in magazines about how marriage is supposed to be, and I never measure up. She thinks I'm a lousy husband.

"Last night she told me she wants out of our marriage. I know I've not been the greatest husband, but I feel like she has created some sort of fantasy world that really doesn't exist."

It didn't matter to this man that cars were rushing by or that he was in uniform. At that moment, he was just another hurting husband trying to figure out how to love his wife. But he was in competition with an *image* of a relationship that doesn't really exist.

As his patrol car pulled away, I couldn't help but reflect on our conversation. Here was a guy, less than perfect like all of us, who was losing his marriage to an imaginary world he could not beat. I'll never learn the outcome of his situation, but I do know that no marriage can survive when real-life spouses are pitted against grandiose illusions. President John F. Kennedy said of his older brother, Joseph, who had been killed in battle, that he felt like he was "shadow boxing" with his dead brother. Apparently, no matter how hard Kennedy tried, he didn't feel that he ever measured up to the image of his "perfect" brother.

The state police officer was in the ring, shadow boxing with a fantasy he couldn't knock out. Living in a dreamworld won't get your needs met, and it won't help your marriage get better. I promise.

FRIENDSHIPS WITH THE OPPOSITE SEX

In talking about the wrong places we turn for love and affection, we must look at opposite-sex friendships. We can't hide our head in the sand. Opposite-sex interaction is a part of life, and at times friendships develop as a result of working with and interacting with people of the opposite sex. That's perfectly normal as long as these relationships are kept at a cordial but careful distance.

Married people who haven't experienced the problems that can come from this situation may think I'm making a big deal out of nothing, but those who have lived with an opposite-sex friendship gone awry know the pain and risk that it can create.

If you're starved for affection, opposite-sex friendships make you particularly vulnerable to marital disaster. If you find yourself having more in common with and enjoying more time with a friend of the opposite sex than with your spouse, the seeds for marital destruction have been planted and will likely grow if watered even a little bit. One of my former coworkers and a longtime friend, Dr. Todd Linaman, has made important contributions to the understanding of the vulnerability and dangers of opposite-sex friendships. I've included some of his excellent work throughout this chapter, including the following list of twenty questions.

How do you know if an opposite-sex friendship poses a potential threat to your marriage? It does if you or your spouse honestly answer yes to any of the following twenty questions:

1. Is your spouse unaware of your opposite-sex friendship?

2. Would you behave differently around your friend if your spouse were present?

3. Would you feel uncomfortable if your spouse had the same quality of friendship with someone of the opposite sex as you do?

4. Do you prefer to spend time alone with your opposite-sex friend rather than in a group setting?

5. Are you physically and/or emotionally attracted to your friend?

6. Is your friend someone you would consider dating if you were single?

7. Have you ever entertained romantic fantasies about your friend?

8. Do you ever compare your spouse with your friend?

9. Do you think about sharing important news with your friend before your spouse?

10. Do you and your friend ever exchange highly personal details about your lives or complain about your marriages to each other?

11. Do you often reference or talk about your friend with others?

12. Has your spouse ever expressed concern about your friendship?

13. Is your relationship with your friend ever a source of tension or conflict between you and your spouse?

14. Have you ever ignored or minimized your spouse's requests to end or modify the relationship with your friend?

15. Have you ever deceived or misled your spouse about matters concerning your friendship?

16. Has anyone other than your spouse ever cautioned you about your opposite-sex friendship?

17. Do you do things with your friend that your spouse is unwilling or uninterested in doing?

18. Does your friend fulfill needs that you wish your spouse would meet?
19. Do you have unexpressed or unresolved anger toward your spouse?
20. Does your marriage lack intimacy?

WHAT CAN YOU DO?

If you or your spouse answered yes to any of the questions above, you must act now to protect your marriage.

You can't hide from people of the opposite sex simply because you're feeling a lack of affection in your marriage. But—whether or not you're having marital difficulties—married people need to be honest with themselves about the nature of relationships they have with those of the opposite sex. We know that friendship is the basis of romantic love, so if you find yourself developing a stronger friendship with a person of the opposite sex than what you have with your own spouse, you may be setting yourself up for something more than just a friendship.

Eight ways to manage opposite-sex friendships while strengthening your marriage

We've heard the stories about watercooler or lunchtime romances when coworkers of the opposite sex start talking about their problems. One thing leads to another, and before you know it there's an affair.

These principles will keep you in safe territory as you deal with members of the opposite sex in the normal course of life and will also work to safeguard and improve your marriage.

The first five are positive steps to build up your marriage, protecting it from vulnerability in opposite-sex friendships.

The last three are pitfalls to avoid as you work on having a more affectionate marriage.

1. *Make your relationship with Christ your number one priority.*

A growing, mature Christian is better equipped to deal with opposite-sex friendships in a healthy way. Her spiritual needs are being met by God; she is absorbing God's Word regularly, shaping her mind to see things God's way; and she understands her sinful nature and the possibility of temptation. A mature Christian will not avoid friendships with people of the opposite sex, but she will recognize areas of potential vulnerability and stay far from the danger line.

By meeting your needs through God and your spouse, you will be strengthened and empowered to keep opposite-sex friendships, wherever they occur, within appropriate boundaries.

2. *Develop and consistently nurture a best-friend relationship with your spouse.*

Studies have shown that most people who consider themselves happily married say the number one ingredient in their marital happiness is a strong friendship between them. Friends share similar interests and do things together. You can be yourself with your best friend. Friends talk about concerns, are trustworthy, and don't gossip about each other. Even though there may be a lack of affection in your marriage, I strongly encourage you to work on those things that can strengthen your friendship.

3. *Address unmet needs and unresolved anger in your marriage.*

The strong marriage where both people are having their

needs for affection met is able to withstand natural attraction and keep opposite-sex friendships at a healthy distance.

By addressing your needs and your spouse's needs for affection, you will not make yourself affair-*proof*—no one is beyond temptation—but you will strengthen your resolve and be less vulnerable. It's like taking vitamins, eating healthy food, and exercising to build up your immune system so it can then better fight off infection. A strong, healthy marriage can better withstand the "infection" of temptation toward unfaithfulness.

Unresolved anger and unmet needs are fuels that drive people toward affairs. They serve as good excuses when you try to justify your wrong behavior by saying, "My wife just isn't meeting my needs" or "My husband just doesn't understand me." It doesn't take much to move from this thinking to being unfaithful.

Nurture your marriage relationship; feed and water it carefully with affection and time spent together so it can grow into a strong and vibrant tree that will better withstand not only temptation, but also the trials that eventually come into every life.

4. Be sure your spouse knows your friend and is completely comfortable with the relationship. If he or she isn't completely comfortable, end the friendship.

Married people should never have an opposite-sex friendship that is hidden from their spouse. Even with no intention of having an affair, people slip from friendship to deep friendship to a sexual relationship because they feel connected and appreciated. They share similar interests. The relationship generally is hidden from the spouse. By being totally open and including your spouse in all of your friendships, you will wisely safeguard your marriage.

5. Be accountable.

If you find yourself in a dangerous friendship with someone of the opposite sex, go to a trusted friend or pastor and ask that they hold you accountable for maintaining appropriate boundaries with that friend. Accountability is an absolute necessity for any growing Christian, whether you feel starved for affection or not. We need each other. God intends for us to hold each another accountable, lift each other up, and encourage each other, as the Bible says in 1 Thessalonians 5:11: "Therefore encourage one another, and build up one another, just as you also are doing" (NASB).

A person who is starved for affection is particularly vulnerable in opposite-sex friendships and needs someone of the same sex who can hold her accountable for her own good and the good of the marriage. The accountability partner must be a solid Christian who is walking closely with God and demonstrating his wisdom in the way she lives her own life. Otherwise, the vulnerable person could receive some unhelpful or even destructive advice.

This person also needs to be able to speak the truth and ask hard questions. While an accountability partner can be a friend, she must be able to push and challenge you. The Bible talks about one person sharpening another like iron sharpens iron (Proverbs 27:17), and this is clearly a part of this process. If your accountability partner simply allows you to complain about your lousy marriage without challenging you to deal with it in a healthy way, she is not the kind of accountability partner you need.

I have talked to people who have progressed from a healthy opposite-sex friendship into an unhealthy one—an affair— where coworkers and friends who saw the signs did nothing and said nothing. Just like friends don't let friends drink and drive, friends don't let friends fall into unhealthy opposite-sex friend-ships without confronting it.

6. Avoid close opposite-sex friendships if you are strug-gling in your marriage relationship or if your friend is strug-gling or seems emotionally needy.

In today's world men and women work together and interact in hundreds of daily settings. This is normal and healthy. But these relationships must be cordial and kept at a careful distance.

We can't and shouldn't totally avoid opposite-sex friend-ships. However, especially if you're struggling in your marriage, it is crucial that you erect clear boundaries around your friend-ships. Don't deliberately seek out friendships with those of the opposite sex.

We read in Proverbs 3:21-23, "My son, preserve sound judg-ment and discernment, do not let them out of your sight; they will be life for you, an ornament to grace your neck. Then you will go on your way in safety, and your foot will not stumble" (NIV). Using discernment in opposite-sex friendships is critical because this is dangerous territory.

Please take some time to evaluate your own friendships with people of the opposite sex. Reread the questions at the beginning of this section and think about your friendships from your spouse's point of view. Ask God for wisdom and dis-cernment in assessing your relationships right now. Do you have a friendship that could prove harmful to your marriage and could develop into something it shouldn't? Even if you aren't emotionally or physically attracted to the friend and your spouse is comfortable with the relationship, evaluate the emotional condition of your opposite-sex friend. Does he or she have needs, or expectations, or vulnerabilities that could lead to further involvement?

Interaction with both men and women happens every day, but the prudent married person avoids developing close friendships with those of the opposite sex. If you're starved for affection, this is even more important.

7. Avoid a close friendship with anyone to whom you are physically or emotionally attracted.

Attraction is a powerful human reaction, usually based on emotional or physical responses. Research reveals that children are more likely to respond to a "pretty" face than they are to others and that attractive people receive warmer receptions during job interviews. Physical attraction is a powerful force between human beings.

People generally prefer to spend time with a person to whom they are emotionally attracted. This makes perfect sense, but it can also create a vulnerable blind spot for a person who is starved for affection.

The key is being honest with yourself. Do you respond positively to someone of the opposite sex with whom you work or attend church? Trust your instincts and your feelings. If you realize that you could become attracted to this person, step away from the friendship—your marriage could be placed at risk. Remember, affairs don't usually begin in the bedroom. They begin in the office, the church, or the neighborhood. They begin in the mind, the unguarded mind that allows itself to pursue an attraction. We must take seriously the warning of Proverbs 4:23, "Above all else, guard your heart, for it is the wellspring of life" (NIV).

8. Avoid close friendships with opposite-sex singles.

I've had a number of calls on my radio program where a wife has expressed concern that her husband has taken on a single mother and her children as a "mission project." In and of itself this is a good idea, but it becomes a problem if he cuts his wife out of the equation. The callers all shared a feeling of being left out and threatened in their relationship. In each case the wife was very concerned that a line had been crossed and her spouse was using the cover of being a "concerned Christian" to meet an emotional need in his life inappropriately.

I advise couples that helping single mothers (or single fathers) and their children is a great ministry for married couples, but it needs to be done only as a couple and not by either spouse alone with the single parent. By helping together, the bond between a husband and wife will be strengthened. But if the couple is not committed to doing it together, it could be dangerous to their marriage.

WHAT IF YOUR SPOUSE WON'T LET GO?

We've talked about ways to strengthen your marriage against the temptation of affairs and ways to avoid pitfalls in opposite-sex friendships. But what if you're married to someone who refuses to end an unhealthy opposite-sex friendship?

Many people have told me that their spouse refuses to cut off an emotional affair. When a strong emotional bond is formed with a person of the opposite sex outside marriage, thinking and priorities become blurred. "What's the harm in e-mailing someone?" a wife may ask. But if her spouse isn't comfortable with her correspondence or personal friendship with someone of the opposite sex, the right thing to do is stop it. Marriage is our number one priority after our relationship with God.

If your spouse refuses to end a relationship with someone of the opposite sex, you must first be sure your reaction is appropriate to the situation and not due to overneediness on your part (we'll discuss this at length in chapter 5). Make sure you're not struggling with your own insecurities and creating a story or a situation that doesn't really exist between your spouse and someone else. Express your concern to a trusted Christian counselor or a strong, godly friend to get some honest feedback about your motives.

If after honest self-assessment, you believe your spouse is involved in an inappropriate friendship and is unwilling to end it, you must address the situation firmly and directly with clear expectations of what is acceptable.

Research is clear that strong marriages confront problems quickly. You can start by suggesting that you and your spouse take the quiz at the beginning of this chapter and talk honestly about any of the questions either of you answered with a yes. If your spouse is unwilling to take the quiz with you, ask him or her to take it alone and really give it some thought because it is a concern for you. If you approach your spouse in a calm and loving manner, free from anger and accusation, you'll most likely achieve the results you desire.

Opposite-sex friendships are fine if they are wholesome, aboveboard, and involve both spouses, but they are definitely a wrong place to look, even unconsciously, for affection. You must thoroughly understand and carefully manage the relationship in order to avoid the snare of an affair.

DON'T GIVE UP

I first saw him eating a Thanksgiving meal at the local rescue mission. Like so many of the homeless there that morning, this man had not weathered the stresses of being on the streets well. His shaggy, dirty beard matched the rest of his body. The clothes he grabbed from a mission clothing box did a good job of hiding his thin frame, but his two beanpole legs were clearly visible, extending about five inches beyond the bottom of his pants.

He was no different from the hundreds of other men and women who had come in off the street for a warm meal. He had a family somewhere who probably wondered where things had gone wrong for him; maybe even a wife and children.

The mission director told me the man's story. "He wasn't always on the streets. He used to be a very successful professional back east. He had a good job and family, but something went wrong and this man gave up on life. The problems were too big, the effort too hard, and he figured the best way of coping would be to abandon ship. He simply gave up on himself and his family and hit the streets. He's been out here ever since." He had been on the streets for years, wandering from coast to coast as the seasons passed. Getting by . . . but never getting anywhere.

I could imagine this man picking up the phone and reconnecting with his family and colleagues. But until he took the first step, nothing good was going to happen for him.

Perhaps you've become homeless without ever leaving your home. You've given up on ever receiving the kind of affection you need. There comes a point when giving up on a relationship may seem like the only reasonable choice. But in doing so, you end up hurting yourself even more than the one you love. Giving in to discouragement is not the best road to travel. Making changes in your marriage is healthy, but giving up on your marriage isn't.

When Jacob called me, he was on the verge of giving up on his relationship with Gail. He *could* have, and probably would have had the support of his friends and family. They knew he wasn't happy, had watched him give the marriage a go, and could see that it wasn't working out. Thankfully, instead of doing something stupid, Jacob did something smart—he decided to work on his marriage. He took responsibility for his own behavior and actions and for meeting his needs inappropriately, and he decided to try to nourish his marriage. He didn't give up!

There are many *wrong* ways to meet your needs: looking in the wrong places, fantasizing, demanding, threatening, taking whatever crumbs you can get, and giving up. The *right* way begins when you take responsibility for meeting your needs in a healthy way. Let's see what that looks like and how to do it.

Chapter 5

WHEN IT'S NEVER ENOUGH

Imagine your need for love and affection as the gasoline tank in your car. Is your tank way down on empty with the gauge light blinking and saying, *Stop and get some gas before you die?* Or is it overflowing with love?

Maybe you have one of those huge tanks that takes a lot of fuel to keep full. It's like a big SUV that fills up at the gas station, but five miles down the road it's registering empty again. How about your love tank? Does it feel like the more that's poured into it, the more it leaks out? Does it seem like you can never get enough love?

Or maybe you've got one of those little Volkswagen tanks, holding ten gallons or less. If so, you may have a hard time understanding why your spouse seems to need so much affection.

How full—or empty—is your love tank on a scale of one to ten?

In terms of genuine and satisfying affection in marriage, only your spouse can really provide the high octane fuel you need. The key is obtaining your affection from the right source and in the right proportions. Sometimes spouses fill their tanks with pretty low octane fuel from the wrong source, as when they develop an emotional connection with someone of the opposite sex besides their spouse. That's like filling your tank with dangerous fuel that will eventually explode, unleashing harm and damage all around. We talked about the dangers of opposite-sex friendships in chapter 4.

But what is the right amount? How much is enough? It's not unusual for one spouse to need more affection than another. But sometimes this moves into unhealthy neediness. Being married to a needy person—or *being* a needy person—can be very frustrating. This chapter is designed to give you an understanding of unhealthy neediness and practical strategies for dealing with it. A needy person:

1. Continually seeks feedback on his behavior.
2. Has difficulty accepting a compliment or praise.
3. Demands constant attention.
4. Demonstrates unreasonable jealousy.
5. Is rarely content with herself or others.
6. Has few friendships or interests other than his spouse.
7. Often seeks attention in unhealthy ways such as moodiness, emotional outbursts, extreme shyness, or promiscuity.

TO STAY OR NOT TO STAY

Sarah considered herself a high-need wife with a large love tank. "We just don't come together intimately enough in my opinion—physically," she told me.

She asked what I thought about her taking some time away from the marriage with the goal of reconciliation. I said that separation is always potentially dangerous. When you're in an uncomfortable situation, and you decide to take a break from it for a while, you think, *Why do I ever want to go back into that again when I'm doing okay out here?*

If there's going to be a separation, I always recommend it be done under good counsel with structure and rules involved. For example, while we're separated, we agree there's not going to be any outside dating. We're going to separate for the purpose of really working on the relationship and we'll hold ourselves accountable to a process so we don't get sidetracked with our new feelings. The goal for the separation should always be to reconcile or restore the relationship. People sometimes think, *If I could just dump this guy (or girl) and get with someone else, I'd be happier.* It happens a lot. When needs aren't being met, the tendency may be to just move on instead of really trying to address the issues in a healthy way.

But these same people often find that running away doesn't solve problems. Unless issues are aired and dealt with, you'll probably experience the same type of unsatisfying relationship again and again. Changing partners is not the answer.

Of course, it's a different matter if there's obvious physical danger or serious emotional danger for yourself or your children. Then, separation is for survival.

WHAT'S YOUR GIVING STYLE?

I've observed four basic approaches to relationships that must be understood if we're to find contentment in marriage.

1. I give to get, also known as *manipulation.* The manipulative relationship has conditions attached, and the flow of love can quickly be turned off when and if the manipulative person isn't getting his way. In working with couples, I've seen this phenomenon over and over. During the dating period there's a free exchange of love, affection, and care between both individuals, and their love tanks are full. These feelings of love lead to a decision to get married, but often the couple is unaware that one or both may be needy individuals, incapable of or unwilling to maintain the "loving" feelings throughout the marriage.

2. I give if I get, also known as *withholding love* in order to exert control. The controller's goal is to stay in charge to get what she wants from the other person. It's quite common for a controller to be attracted to an unhealthy pleaser and this must be confronted in the relationship. If this goes unchecked, it leads to an erosion of affection and love over time.

Wanting to please our spouse is a normal, healthy, and positive thing, unless you are always trying to please out of fear of his anger or in order to feel comfortable with yourself, no matter what you have to sacrifice in order to please.

An approach to pleasing is to think of other people's needs and be willing to set some of your own needs aside to help someone who is struggling. An unhealthy pleaser is someone who has to please to feel like she's a worthwhile person or to feel accepted in a relationship. He sacrifices his needs and desires—and often resents it—out of an unhealthy drive to always meet another's needs. He becomes a doormat and then wonders why he's always being stepped on.

3. I don't give, but I expect to get anyway, which is pure *selfishness*. Spouses can get worn out being married to a selfish person who thinks primarily of his own interests and needs and is oblivious to the needs of others, including those closest to him. Selfishness can become pathological when mental illness manifests itself in extreme selfishness with no regard for others whatsoever. Selfishness is sin, pure and simple, but people with mental illnesses, like those with physical maladies, need medical help and treatment.

4. I simply give, which is *love*. The best description of this kind of person can be found in 1 Corinthians 13, commonly known as the "love chapter" of the Bible. Living these principles of love will yield healthy, vibrant, affection-filled marriages.

If you are in a marriage built on manipulation, control, or selfishness, you will need to do two things:

First, study 1 Corinthians 13 and apply that kind of love to your marriage, whether or not you think your spouse deserves it. Be patient, kind, not jealous, humble, not taking into account a wrong suffered, rejoicing with the truth, hoping all things. Read the chapter again and again and put it into action every chance you get.

Second, gain the skills and take the initiative to lovingly confront your spouse about his or her manipulation, control, or selfishness. Talking to a counselor or pastor can help you figure out the best way to do this.

NEEDS—WE ALL HAVE 'EM

Healthy couples recognize the difference between healthy and unhealthy needs. God made us with what I like to call *biblically appropriate* needs. Healthy needs include the need:

1. *to be understood*. When you know who I am and why I do what I do, you "get" me. You know how I think and talk and what motivates me.
2. *to be accepted for who I am without criticism*. Even though I have flaws, you still like and love me. You know I'm

not perfect, but that's okay with you. You know
I extend the same leniency to you as well.

3. *to be loved.* I know I can count on you to share in my
victories and sorrows, no matter what. I know you want
what is best for me.

4. *for affection, closeness, and intimacy.* I feel the warmth
of your concern and care. I know I can tell you anything
and you'll understand. I can be myself with you, without
pretense.

5. *to feel safe from emotional, physical, or spiritual harm.*
I trust you to be kind and good to me, to act in my best
interests, to respect me as a child of God.

All these needs should be met within the bounds of a Christian (biblically appropriate) marriage, which is one where both spouses try to live as God describes in the Bible. Any needs that are not being met clearly indicate a problem. In a biblically appropriate marriage, where both spouses know how to give and take, these normal needs will be met. No marriage is perfect, so there will be times when each of you might feel like you aren't receiving what you require, but for the most part each spouse's needs will be taken care of.

WHERE TO GET A FILL-UP

When I say that both spouses take responsibility for their own needs, what I mean is that no spouse can meet *all* of another person's needs because our deepest need is for God and a relationship with him through Jesus Christ. The apostle Paul expressed it well in Philippians 4:12-13 while writing from prison: "I know how to be abased, and I know how to abound. Everywhere and in all things I have learned both to be full and to be hungry, both to abound and to suffer need. I can do all things through Christ who strengthens me." Whether we're in a satisfying marital relationship or one that leaves much to be desired, we need to turn to God to meet our needs. We know that even in a terrible situation, we can do all things through Christ.

If we expect our spouse to meet *all* of our needs, we are making that person into our god, and that is wrong. The Bible talks about the community of believers, the body of Christ (Romans 12:4-5). God designed us to be in wholesome relationships with more people than just our spouse. Your spouse isn't supposed to meet your needs for friends and family, for hobbies, education, meaningful work, and everything else. Each of us is responsible for meeting our needs in biblically appropriate, healthy ways, and that includes having friends and interests in addition to your marriage. No one, no matter how loving or affectionate, can meet *all* the needs of another person, especially needs that are intended to be met in God, or other people or interests.

Having an oversized love tank is not all bad, but make sure you fill it from the right source instead of expecting it to be filled completely by your spouse. God can fill a love tank the size of the Grand Canyon, and we must go to him with our deepest needs.

Paige has learned that God alone can meet all of her needs. She said, "I have a pretty full love tank because I choose to have joy. I am single now, but I know that until you have oneness with Christ, you'll never have oneness in marriage. Getting up in the morning, I go by [my paraphrase of] Isaiah 60:1—'Rise and shine for the light has come.' You can choose joy.

"I was disowned and disinherited by my parents because of my marriage choice. I went out on a limb thinking my husband knew the Lord, but he didn't. I was battered by that husband, went through a divorce, and then I was raped by a neighbor.

But God never forsook me in any of this. He stood by me. Sometimes I questioned where he was, and he probably questioned where I was. But Christ was my life. He gave us the example in the garden when he said, 'Because of the joy set before me, I can continue' (Hebrews 12:2). It's not looking at your circumstances; it's looking at that joy before you.

"One of the best compliments to me as a Christian came years ago when a fellow employee said when she heard the song, 'I Choose Joy,' she thought of me because she knew all I'd been through."

The emotional damage Paige experienced from her parents' rejection, her husband's abuse, and her neighbor's crime is almost incalculable. But her story illustrates the beauty of turning to God to meet your needs. If he can satisfy this wounded woman, certainly he can meet your needs and heal your wounds as well.

SYMPTOMS OF NEEDINESS

Unhealthy needs include:

1. *Focusing primarily on only one person in the relationship*—what he needs, what he wants, his career, his interests.
2. *Increasing isolation.* A person's world gets smaller and smaller as friends and other appropriate and healthy interests are dropped so that all attention can be focused on the spouse's needs and desires.
3. *Inability to delay gratification.* We live in a time when people want what they want *now*. If they can't wait, that uncomfortable feeling creates anxiety, which often gets filled in unhealthy ways by drugs, alcohol, promiscuity, emotional outbursts, or withdrawal. A healthy life

requires feeling uncomfortable from time to time, whether that means feeling hungry when you're trying to avoid overeating or feeling tired while you're exercising to improve your physical health. Self-discipline includes discomfort, but that can be a good, normal, and healthy experience. Don't expect your marriage to heal overnight. By putting in the work and effort described in this book, you will nourish your marriage. But it's not a matter of instant gratification—it takes time.

4. *Demanding your own way.* We talked earlier about selfishness and how it's not part of God's design for marriage. When we demand our own way, we are not taking responsibility for meeting our own needs. By expecting others to jump when we have a need or desire, we give the impression that we are more important than those we want to "serve" us and our needs.

5. *Being overly dependent on your spouse* to the point where he or she almost defines who you are. You have few interests of your own, your thoughts are constantly on what your spouse will think or do, you anticipate his moods and act to avoid upsetting him. This is often called codependency, as it describes someone who is hooked into another person and her problems and in effect loses his separate identity.

THE RESULTS OF NEEDINESS

If you're married to a needy person who is never filled, or if you are a needy person yourself, it can create a variety of painful and difficult emotions and experiences in the relationship. Through my experience I have observed the following:

1. *Resentment* toward the person who either is not meeting your needs or who is draining you by his or her unmeetable needs.
2. *Loss of respect*, which is a marriage killer. The Bible tells wives to respect their husbands. I have found that when a man loses the respect of his wife, it becomes the seed of great bitterness, distance, and destruction.
3. *Withdrawal*. When a person can't change something, he often gets discouraged and pulls back into his shell.
4. *Anger*, which can either go underground and come out as depression or anxiety, or be overt with outbursts and game-playing.
5. *Emotional, spiritual, or physical problems* like overeating, overworking, or overdoing other activities to try to meet needs that are not being addressed in the marriage relationship.

Being married to a needy spouse is a double-edged sword because the ultra-needy person is never satisfied and will often try to fill his needs in unhealthy ways. This then creates resentment, loss of respect, and withdrawal on the part of the person who doesn't feel like he or she can ever do enough.

FORMULA FOR DISAPPOINTMENT

I use the abbreviation E-R=D (*Expectations minus Reality equals Disappointment*) to represent the heart of many problems in relationships. If you're not happy with your marriage, your kids, your job, or even your faith, it's because the expectations you have minus the reality of life is resulting in disappointment.

For example, if we expect God to be a genie in a bottle who will meet all of our needs, wishes, and desires including health, wealth, and prosperity, we're sure to be disappointed when we don't always get what we want.

But if we build our expectations on scriptural teaching, we find that the purpose of our life is to serve God and enjoy an intimate relationship with him and others, not necessarily to be healthy, wealthy, or wise, although often God blesses us with some of those things, too.

It is biblically appropriate for men and women in marriage to give and receive affection freely. This includes a satisfying sexual relationship, an ability to discuss and resolve problems, freedom from abuse or neglect, and equal value placed on both spouses. Those are all biblically appropriate and reasonable expectations.

On the other hand, if we're focusing on unhealthy and abnormal needs, such as self-focus or demanding our own way, we'll continue to live a life of disappointment.

If you're married to a person who is unwilling or incapable of giving or receiving love, then it would be healthy for you to make some reasonable adjustments to your expectations, and to take steps to meet your needs in suitable ways: in healthy relationships with friends and family; with interests in hobbies, work, or education; and most important, in a vibrant relationship with God. In order to survive in that kind of marriage relationship, you must make reasonable adjustments in your expectations so you're not waking up every morning disappointed and constantly beating your head against the wall.

You can't change another person, but you can change yourself. You can change your expectations to reflect reality, you can take steps to meet your needs in healthy ways, and you can increase your level of contentment and satisfaction.

Alan talked to me about changing his expectations to reflect reality. He said, "We dated for about a year and a half before we married twenty years ago and then waited another two years before we had children. We were careful before we were married to avoid getting involved physically. I'm glad we didn't have premarital sex because that brings problems into a marriage.

"But now we're having problems because something terrible happened to my wife when she was a child and it messed her up real bad. She hasn't told me what it is yet, but we don't have sex very often, only once every couple of years. She's getting counseling and she's trying to deal with it constantly. There was a year where sex was nonstop for us, but as her past caught up with her, it started taking her down, and I watched it. But I married her because I love her, not for affection, and I leave the lack of affection in our marriage in God's hands."

Alan described the way his wife has stood by him during sickness, making him want to stand by her now during her struggle. He said they are close in other ways, sharing with each other, holding hands, and being committed.

"We have good communication, and even when I'm tempted outside the marriage, we talk it all out and it works out better. And you need self-esteem. Ephesians 5:21 says to submit yourself one to another, and it's not genderizing it as men. It's just telling people to submit to one another pretty much as you are gifted, is the way I interpret it. My wife has gifts I just don't have, like handling our finances and raising our children. So I let her have the run of those areas because I'm not as gifted and we fall behind if I get in charge.

"The hardest struggle is against yourself. If you can get yourself in line, then you'll do a lot better."

Alan has found contentment and patience. While the amount or type of affection in his marriage isn't what he wishes it were, he focuses on the positives and continually renews his commitment to his wife. As he talked, I heard hope in his voice. He has accepted the reality of his situation, but he knows God can repair the damage and restore the affection he desires in his marriage. Alan's expectations are realistic and also hopeful.

KING BABY

Some adults are little people in big bodies. If you're married to an emotionally and spiritually immature person, it can be exasperating. You can't force another person to grow up, but you certainly don't have to enable that person to continue irresponsible and immature behaviors. The same principles that we would use in disciplining a teenager sometimes need to be applied in our marriage, using the respectful approach of logical and natural consequences that come from a spouse's (or a teen's) immature behavior.

Sometimes immaturity is due to childhood experiences, and understanding your childhood experiences can be a powerful tool, as we talked about in chapter 3. The way your spouse remembers childhood—the words and emotions attached to those memories—reveal a great deal about how she views life today. Some people get emotionally stuck in childhood and never grow up.

Being the baby of my family, when I married Donna I expected her to pick up where my mother had left off. As a child, if I took off my clothes, they were picked up. If I skinned my knee, I got an Oreo cookie. When I got married, I realized that my wife's job wasn't to pick up my clothes and hang them back up. It took some time over the years, but she helped me to grow up and become more mature as a husband. This is something we need to learn to do with each other. Sometimes it takes a little confrontation, a little iron sharpening iron, but the bottom line is that we cannot foster or encourage immature behavior in healthy marriages.

It's not that we refuse to help our spouse or children, but we don't carry their load in doing things for them they should be doing for themselves. We don't accept mistreatment and allow them to keep doing it to their detriment and ours. Just as a teen learns about consequences when his expensive bike is left out during a storm, a spouse who overspends or fails to keep commitments must learn that what they do or don't do creates consequences in their life.

Unfortunately, some people never grow up spiritually or emotionally. When parents look at their six-month-old baby who is cooing and crying and smiling, they're excited. *Isn't he cute?* But if that baby was actually five years old but still behaving like a six-month-old, his parents would rightfully be concerned—that's not normal.

While everyone goes through stages of growth and development, if our maturity has been arrested at some point, it's a serious problem that must be addressed, often with outside help from a Christian counselor or pastor. That's why I do what I do on my radio program every day—I want to help people grow up and live authentic Christian lives in their relationships and to mature and be what God wants them to be.

WHAT CAN I DO?

Our goal as mature spouses is to seek a healthy balance. First, we must be sure we understand what a biblically appropriate need for affection looks like. Then we must adjust for individual personalities and preferences and find a range that is normal. Generally, each spouse should be able to give and receive affection through hand holding, kissing, hugging, conversation, and sexual relations that are comfortable for both.

Second, we need to assess any unhealthy neediness and take steps, either through counseling or mutual understanding, to help the needy spouse find healthy ways to build friendships and interests so that she will have some of her needs met elsewhere.

Realizing that you are overly needy can be an uncomfortable feeling, but discomfort can be used by God to cause change in our life. Instead of seeing the discomfort you're going through as your enemy, look at it as an opportunity for you to really grow. We don't grow as much when things are going well as we do when things are tough. We all know the analogy of a seed dying and going into the ground or iron needing to be melted so it can be shaped into a form that can be used as a tool.

In our culture we want to run away from discomfort. We want a pill or an activity or a relationship—something to take away the discomfort. Many times we rush to heal people before allowing the process of suffering to do its job. We don't like to deal with grief, loss, pain, or discomfort. We rush to feel better, to find instant relief, and to anesthetize the pain.

If you are married to an unhealthy person—perhaps a person who is unable or unwilling to make some changes in himself—sit back and prayerfully try to understand what God is doing here. He often teaches us about ourselves, our needs, and the needs of others when we're going through difficulty. Instead of rushing in to try to change your spouse and make your marriage "better," stop and find out what's going on in your own life.

Do you honestly believe, after reflection, that you are doing your part to meet your spouse's needs? Are you putting effort into your relationship, spending time together, showing affection, sharing conversation? Are you appreciative of what your spouse does for you and your family? Are you sure your wants and desires from your spouse are balanced, that you're not looking to him or her to meet needs that can only be met in God, or other people or interests?

If you want to make a change in your marriage, you have to move from apathy to commitment. One of the greatest enemies of change is complacency. I tell men, in particular, that we often mistake routine for satisfaction. We assume that since there's food on the table and things are going pretty well around the house, there is satisfaction. Until our spouse clearly points out that there is a problem, we assume everything is okay.

One of the best ways to get our love tanks down to a reasonable size is by helping others. You've heard this before, but by doing for others, you get your mind off yourself and your problems. You begin to care about someone else's struggles, and you often find new perspective on your own situation. Don't wait until you have some free time or some extra money to help someone else. By faith, reach out to someone else, and by some odd paradox that our brilliant God conceived, you will get more than you give. It happens every time. The giver finds out that the Bible statement is true: It is more blessed to give than to receive.

And practice thankfulness. Make a list of some of the many things you can thank God for. You'll be surprised that it goes on and on. Make a list of what you are thankful about concerning your spouse. Then express to both God and your spouse how much you appreciate these things, and be specific. Acquiring the habit of being thankful goes a long way in helping our love tanks stay comfortably full. And it breaks down entitlement attitudes that often breed discontentment as we think, *I deserve a better marriage than this. I deserve someone who can meet my needs.*

In reality, what we deserve is eternal death as a result of our sins. God owes us nothing, but he gives us everything we need. Once we realize this, the good things we *do* have will take on new meaning and will provide more satisfaction as we appreciate them.

Yvonne has a needy husband. She said, "My love tank is usually pretty full, and I keep it that way. I have my kids and my friends, and I find enjoyment in them. But my husband feels that his love tank is usually empty. He requires a lot of affection, and I guess I don't require as much. It just drains me because he's so needy. He wants to hug more and for me to reach out to him more, and I feel like I'm constantly doing that or constantly apologizing, or constantly feeling like I need to keep this up. But it's never enough, and I'm mentally exhausted. We are two different people. He doesn't have any friends. His life is work and our kids, and that's it. For me, I work and I have my children and friends I enjoy, so I'm usually pretty happy.

"He said all it would take is just a hug, but when I do that, it's still not enough. I should have done it longer, or he'll say, 'How come you didn't kiss me when you did that?'"

When one spouse has a huge tank and the other spouse has a small spigot pouring into it, it's tough. I suggested that Yvonne, who is a practical, down-to-earth, let's-get-it-done kind of person, try to let her husband know she loves him in a language he can understand, instead of arguing about it.

I told her, "The two of you need to talk about it and come to an agreement on how you're going to show affection to each other. He needs to grow up, and you probably need to understand him a little better."

Unhealthy neediness is a challenge in marriage. It requires

confronting issues, getting counseling, each spouse exploring his or her own needs and taking responsibility for them, honestly assessing one's maturity level, and understanding what the Scripture teaches. It means being willing to feel uncomfortable at times so that we have a chance to grow. But above all, we need to anchor our life in that foundational truth—that ultimately we can always fall back on God, who waits with open arms to meet our deepest needs, as Philippians 4:19 promises, "My God shall supply all your needs according to His riches in glory by Christ Jesus."

HE IS THE REASON

What does all this have to do with being starved for affection? My point here is this: Only *you* can change yourself, and you are the *only* person you can change. You can take action to improve your marriage, and your actions may very well cause changes in your spouse. But none of us can correct the flaws in another person. It just doesn't work that way. We can, however, change ourselves.

Also, in answering the deep questions of why you exist and how you can relate to others in a healthy way, you must realize that, no matter how much you love your spouse, you can't live only for him or her. Only the Creator can give us the ultimate reason to live: to know, love, and serve him. In fact, you'll always be disappointed if you try to have someone else meet a need in your life that only God can fulfill.

In his book *A Purpose-Driven Life*, Rick Warren says, "Most conflict is rooted in unmet needs." Relationship conflicts—at home, in the office, wherever—occur when people don't think that their needs are being met. Scripture clearly backs this up: "What causes fights and quarrels among you? Don't they come from your desires that battle within you? You want something but don't get it. You kill and covet, but you cannot have what you want. You quarrel and fight. You do not have, because you do not ask God" (James 4:1-2, NIV).

When you expect anyone—friend, spouse, boss, or family member—to meet a need that only God can fill, you are setting yourself up for disappointment and bitterness. No one can meet all your needs except God.

YOU CAN DO IT!

We're about to get into specific ways you can get the nourishment back into your marriage. You may be thinking that it takes two to tango and wondering how you can do this alone. The good news is that by implementing the ideas in this book, you can feed your marriage and revive it from its starved and even lifeless state. You can begin to load your marital refrigerator with healthy, nourishing foods that your spouse will eventually want to try.

What if I don't feel like it? you may ask. Maybe you feel like your spouse is the one who should be trying to improve the emotional meals around your house and that you've tried everything you know to do. But I've observed during my years working with people that feelings follow actions. If you *act* loving, over time you will begin to *feel* love. If you *show* affection, you will *grow* affectionate. If you *practice* smiling, over time you will *be* more cheerful. Your feelings can return even if they seem numb now.

Even if you feel like affection starvation is about to wipe you out, I hope you'll be willing to put your faith in the God who can do all things, the God with whom nothing is impossible. Believe that he can and will make a difference for the better in your marriage based on your efforts to try, even if it means try-ing alone. I still believe one person can make a difference, be-cause I've seen it happen time and time again.

Let's get started.

SECTION
TWO

Chapter 6

IT TAKES MORE
THAN LOVE

"I know we still love each other . . . so why have things gone so wrong?"

I've heard that question, or variations of it, hundreds of times over the years, and it truly strikes to the heart of what I want to now explore: the difference between love and affection, and the need for both in marriage. Understanding this difference will prove foundational to transforming your marriage from one that is affection-starved to one that is rich in affection and truly growing in love. If you are the one who's feeling starved for affection in your marriage, understanding this concept will empower you to move ahead to enrich your marriage. And you can move ahead whether or not your partner is willing to join you right now.

I reminded you earlier of God's command to love. When faced with marital troubles, many counselors or authors may simply conclude that all both spouses need to do is love each other more, and everything will work out fine. But I tell couples that *love isn't enough.* Why would I say that? Because a healthy marriage needs affection, and that's something you have to grow into. Affection takes effort. It takes practice.

LOVE AND AFFECTION ARE DIFFERENT

I've repeatedly referred to love and affection separately in this book. That's intentional—because love and affection are *not* the same thing.

Love is a biblical mandate and is foundational to a successful marriage. I'm convinced every reasonably healthy person is equipped to love others the way God designed. You choose to love someone else by putting their needs above your own. It's a commitment of your will.

Affection, however, is a step *beyond* love. Affection takes the loving relationship between a man and woman in marriage into the deeper realm of tender expressions that result in feelings of closeness, passion, and security. Affection takes work because it requires knowledge of what makes the other person tick. You show affection when you perceive and appreciate what your spouse needs and meet those needs in a way he or she can understand. Affection results in marital contentment, intimacy, satisfaction, anticipation, and joy all wrapped into one package.

- Affection isn't sexual, but it naturally leads to sexual satisfaction.
- Affection isn't time, but it requires time to accomplish.
- Affection isn't communication, but without communication there can be no affection.
- Affection isn't romance, but it typically involves romantic spontaneity, creativity, and fun.

Moreover, when affection is present in your relationship, you just know it. If you don't feel it, you probably don't have it. Here's my definition of affection:

Affection is the kind of love that leaves you feeling close, safe, and cared for. In marriage, you feel the passion, and the loving acts become person specific. As we've said, affection is also important between parent and child. An affectionate family makes a child feel close, safe, and cared for as well. Affection must be an ingredient in all healthy personal relationships, including those with friends and extended family.

The Bible describes love in terms of action, not feelings. Look at the familiar description of love from 1 Corinthians 13, and notice all of the actions required:

"Love is patient, love is kind. It does not envy, it does not boast, it is not proud. It is not rude, it is not self-seeking, it is not easily angered, it keeps no record of wrongs. Love does not delight in evil but rejoices with the truth. It always protects, always trusts, always hopes, always perseveres. Love never fails" (1 Corinthians 13:4-8a NIV).

I like to say (though it may be grammatically flawed) that affection is **"love as actions"**—actions that leave your spouse feeling really good about you and your marriage. Affection is one of the outworkings of love: Love is the commitment and the action, and affection is the safe, secure feeling that results. Strong marriages thrive when both the *behavior of love* and the *feelings of affection* are present. This "love as actions" is what moves you the eighteen inches from your head to your heart:

- Love is patient. Affection is empathetic.
- Love is kind. Affection is tender.
- Love is not rude. Affection thoughtfully apologizes for its words.
- Love is not self-seeking. Affection rubs the back of a discouraged spouse.
- Love does not delight in evil. Affection carefully and privately uncovers sin and helps the person back onto his feet.
- Love never fails. Affection undergirds and confirms your unfailing love for your spouse.

I've learned in my own marriage that to display "love as actions" means I need to get behind Donna's eyes and see life from her perspective. What's important to her must be important to me. When I do the dishes without being asked, that's affection to her. When I tell her how attractive she is to me (which she really is, by the way), that's affection to her. I show her affection when I am tender, close, and passionate in those ways that bring *her* pleasure. Let me give a warning here: It's *not* affection when the goal is to fulfill *my own* pleasure.

Best-selling author Dr. Gary Chapman is one of my favorite radio guests. He wrote a book called *The Five Love Languages*. It's popular, in part, because Gary gives the reader the key to understanding another person at a deeper level. Taking the time to understand another person's language of love is, in itself, an intimate act. He breaks love languages into five basic categories: *gifts*, *words of affirmation*, *touch*, *acts of service*, and *quality time*. Discovering your spouse's love language is one step toward being affectionately connected in marriage. When your spouse speaks your language, you feel understood. When she doesn't, you don't.

Diane and her husband read the book together. She told me, "After seventeen years of marriage and a lot of hard work, we realized what each other's love languages are, and we try and take care of that for each other.

"My love language is physical, and his is words of affirmation. When he's holding my hand and just looking into my eyes and talking to me, that means so much to me. And I know leaving notes for him and telling him how much I appreciate that he's fixed the toilet and other things makes him appreciative. If we get caught up with a busy lifestyle and we don't take time for each other and put that into the schedule, we have problems."

Have you identified your primary love language and your

spouse's? Seeing the situation from your spouse's perspective will be a valuable step in understanding what makes your spouse feel loved and appreciated and what acts of affection look like to him.

Let's revisit Denise and Greg from chapter 1. Denise knew that Greg loved her, but it wasn't getting through to her in a way that made her feel loved, and it was this lack of feeling loved—the absence of affection—that mattered to her. I thought it telling when she said, "Greg knew how to *make* love to me, but he forgot how to *love* me." With "love as actions" gone—with affection nonexistent—Denise sought it elsewhere even though, again, she knew Greg still loved her.

"I thought everything was going good for us until Denise announced that she hadn't been happy for months," Greg remembered. "When I discovered she had been involved with another guy on the Internet, I about lost it. I just completely missed catching on to how lonely she had become." Loneliness born, not out of a lack of love, but the absence of affection. Greg had failed to be affectionate toward his wife, and the cost was high.

YOU *ARE* RESPONSIBLE FOR HOW YOUR SPOUSE FEELS

Those of us in the mental health field love our theories, so you've probably heard this one before: "Others can't make you *feel* anything." While I understand the genesis of that statement, I've got to tell you it still leaves me cold. In fact, my response to that psychobabble is—Baloney! I would challenge my learned colleagues to try and sell that nonsense to the real people I talk to each day with real problems and genuine pain.

Who makes the wife of a physically abusive husband feel afraid and angry? Does she do it to herself? How about the frustrated mother of three preschool children just coming off a week of sleepless nights with a colicky baby? Before telling her, "Honey, you shouldn't feel that way," you better be close to an exit. Enter the quiet halls of a hospice where you find an elderly man bent over the bedside of his dying wife and try to convince him that he is *choosing* to feel devastated. I can almost see him now as he glares right through you, revealing the pain and loss that only a loving husband of fifty-four years can understand. Or consider the young college coed, who just last night was ravaged by a rapist outside her apartment near the university. Are her fears of her own doing?

Technically, my trained counselor side acknowledges that ultimately each individual is responsible for his feelings. But in the real world, people affect people, and those unwanted feelings of anger, fear, and frustration occur because of our vulnerability to relationships. We can't snap our fingers and make the feelings go away. It's the reality of our effect on each other that makes one relationship a joy and another a pain.

Let me ask you, how do you feel when your spouse:

- ignores you?
- cuts you off when you talk?
- criticizes you in front of others?
- refuses sex?
- confuses intimacy with sex?
- ridicules your faith?
- spends more time with others than with you?
- ignores the children?
- overspends, even after you have agreed to cut back?

Each person in a marriage needs to think about how his or her affectionate actions—or lack thereof—impact the other. By taking responsibility for showing *love as actions*, you can consistently influence your spouse in a positive way.

MALE AND FEMALE PERSPECTIVES

In order to express affection, you must be able to experience your emotions, something that is difficult for many people, especially men. God made some people to be "thinkers" who are primarily led by their thoughts, and others to be "feelers" who are strongly influenced by their emotions. We talked in chapter 4 about the need to keep our emotions in check so that we're not ruled by out-of-control feelings, but there's an opposite situation as well where our emotions go unused and ignored.

Donna never saw me cry until one night in 1994. While I'm not proud of that fact, it is true. We had been married almost twenty-four years. Our marriage hadn't required lots of emotional maintenance, but that changed in one night. I was forty-one years old, and my emotional awakening came as a surprise.

I had stood for several weeks over my father's unconscious body. While holding his hand, I watched as he took his last breath. After his death, I became preoccupied with helping my mother pull together all the required details. I was hurting and numb, but in control . . . for the moment.

You need to understand that my dad was my hero. When I needed to talk, he was there. When I sought counsel, he gave it. When I desired encouragement, he provided it. He had gone through years of tough medical procedures and had been near death before, but had always pulled out of it. This time, however, was different. My beloved dad was really gone.

About a week after the funeral, my emotions started to build. I could feel them welling up, and I did my best to control them. But the intensity of the pain and loss was about to reach a critical point, and I couldn't ignore it any longer. Emotional momentum was at its peak. Finally, the force of the feelings exceeded my capacity to hold them back. Without notice they came. In the darkness of the night they came. Awakening me from sleep they came.

I had no control over what was happening, and I didn't like it. This situation was a scary thing for someone like me who prided himself on keeping his cool. For the first time in my adult life, I had lost control of my feelings.

My trembling and crying startled Donna awake; this behavior was highly unusual for me. She put her arms around me and quietly said that things were going to be okay. As a counselor, I was used to being around out-of-control people. In fact, it was my job to help my clients experience a breakthrough, which often makes them vulnerable to their feelings. But experiencing that "breakthrough" myself was another thing entirely.

I share this for those of you who, like me, have difficulty expressing emotions; and for those who, unlike me, don't understand why some people can't just let it out. From personal experience, I can tell you that it takes time, and sometimes it requires a terrible crisis to awaken your emotional life.

I've come a long way since 1994, and I've made huge strides toward emotional freedom. In fact, even as I'm typing the story of my dad's death right now, the emotions are very near. They are warm, happy, and hopeful feelings. My feelings allow me to enjoy the great memories, the good days, and the positive thoughts. I still miss spending time with my dad and talking things over with him. My greatest regret, though, was that it took a crisis to awaken my emotions.

Many of the Bible's leading characters had strong emotions, and they knew how to express them openly and with conviction:

- 🎴 **Nehemiah** felt the people's need, and he went on to rebuild the broken-down walls of Jerusalem. Look at his honest, transparent emotional reaction to the plight of his homeland: "When I heard these things, I sat down and wept. For some days I mourned and fasted and prayed before the God of heaven" (Nehemiah 1:4, NIV).

- 🎴 **Joseph** experienced such anguish and pain at the hands of his brothers that when he met up with them again, all his raw emotion was brought to the surface: "Then Joseph could no longer control himself before all his attendants, and he cried out, 'Have everyone leave my presence!' So there was no one with Joseph when he made himself known to his brothers. And he wept so loudly that the Egyptians heard him, and Pharaoh's household heard about it" (Genesis 45:1-2, NIV).

- 🎴 **David** grieved so deeply over his dying son that no one in his kingdom could comfort him: "David pleaded with God for the child. He fasted and went into his house and spent the nights lying on the ground. The elders of the household stood beside him to get him up from the ground, but he refused, and he would not eat any food with them" (2 Samuel 12:16-17, NIV).

- 🎴 The prophet **Jeremiah** agonized so profoundly over the spiritual condition of Judah that he has been termed the "weeping prophet." "Oh, my anguish, my anguish! I writhe in pain. Oh, the agony of my heart! My heart pounds within me, I cannot keep silent. For I have heard the sound of the trumpet; I have heard the battle cry" (Jeremiah 4:19, NIV).

Learning to recognize and feel your own emotions can help you recognize how your spouse *feels* in response to difficulty and trial, and then discover how you can show affection in a way that will identify with those feelings and therefore be truly meaningful. It's one of the most significant ways you can display "love as actions" to your spouse.

IT'S NORMAL TO *FEEL*

As a counselor and radio show host, I've found that the question of "normalcy" is a big deal with people. What's normal? Who's normal? A fully functioning, normal person can brush up against her daily world without bringing home, at day's end, a bag of hurt feelings. Likewise, a fully functioning, normal person doesn't conclude his day with no feeling at all.

There's a balance between the two extremes, but there's no doubt that normal, healthy people *feel*. Normal, healthy marriages *feel*. And normal, healthy people are affected by others.

- Despite being the all-powerful Son of God, Jesus wept for his people. He grieved over the death of Lazarus; and he celebrated with the bride and groom at the wedding of Cana.
- Despite being one of Jesus' apostles, Peter feared certain people.
- Despite being a prophet called directly by God, Jonah despised certain people.
- Despite offering the pleasing sacrifices to God, Abel was hated by his brother, Cain.

These are just a few examples from the Bible; its pages are filled with normal, healthy people who could feel.

An abnormal marriage, on the other hand, is one without appropriate feelings. It is operating outside God's plan for relationships. Some of these elements may be present:

- put-downs—both privately or in front of others
- abuse of any kind—physical, emotional, spiritual
- criticism—verbal and nonverbal
- manipulation of any kind—emotional, financial, physical
- lack of touching
- regular mention or threats of divorce
- pornography or other addictions
- workaholism
- an overfocus on the children
- distrust—the breaking of a confidence

MANAGING YOUR EMOTIONS

While it's normal and healthy to "feel" or experience your emotions, feelings must be managed or controlled if they're not to get the better of you. The work you want to do to improve your marriage and bring both of you back to the table will be much easier to do if you have your emotions under management, if not under control.

Jennifer immediately identified herself as being starved for affection when she called my radio show. Just from hearing her voice, I could tell she was the type of person who wore her emotions on her sleeve. "I have always struggled with my emotions," she admitted, "but things are particularly bad now. Why can't my spouse just show me the affection I need? Is it that difficult for him to stop being so selfish and start paying a little attention to me?"

Her frustration was apparent as she said that for months she had been stuck on the tracks of an emotional roller coaster. One day she'd be fiercely angry with her husband. The next she would slide into depression.

Remember the proverb, "Hope deferred makes the heart sick" (Proverbs 13:12)? This little verse could be placed on a banner and hung over the door to the next meeting of the "starved for affection" support group because its members know what it's like to continually hope, day after day, for the affection that seldom arrives. While this sickness of heart takes different forms, anger is the most common result. But anger won't help you get what you need.

Perhaps you grew up in a home where expressions of anger were discouraged or simply not allowed, and now you find your feelings of anger troubling or condemning. Or maybe your angry outbursts are a problem in your marriage. In either extreme, it's important that the affection-starved person manages anger appropriately.

When you're starved for affection and closeness in your marriage, the myriad of feelings like anger that you're likely to experience should come as no surprise, especially if you tend to be a person led by your emotions. But you can turn your emotions into a valuable ally. Instead of letting your feelings drag you down, you can pick yourself up and take action instead.

These actions will help keep your emotions in check:

- *Keep a regular journal of your feelings.* Journaling is helpful since it requires your mind to organize its thoughts before your hand can write them down. This mental process of arranging your thoughts can work wonders in calming your spirit. If writing isn't your thing, then dictate your feelings and thoughts onto a tape recorder for later playback.

- *Find healthy outlets for personal development.* As you grow personally through acts of service, education, community and church involvement, your thoughts are diverted from the constant reminder of "what's wrong" in your relationship. Personal development is not an attempt to deny the realities of a troubled relationship but an opportunity to allow for more balance in your life.
- *Develop and maintain a routine.* As simple as this suggestion appears, it's perhaps the most important and most difficult to accomplish. By keeping your physical, spiritual, and emotional life intact and your home and personal world organized, balanced, and moving, you will actually lessen the negative impact that comes from lacking affection.
- *Get regular physical exercise.* A half hour a day spent walking, running, or exercising in another way can help your mood. Ask your doctor before beginning any new exercise program.

These activities will help you achieve your personal goals in your marriage and in every other area of your life, as you learn to function with balance and calmness.

The good news is that out-of-control feelings can be reigned in; abnormal can become normal; dead marriages can come to life; and starved marriages can become full. Married couples were designed by God to experience feelings of affection, closeness, and intimacy in marriage.

The biblical ideal is for your marriage to be filled with both love *and* affection, and this book has been written to help you achieve that in your own marriage. Keep reading!

Chapter 7

FROM FAMINE
TO FEAST

A vibrant, affectionate marriage is built on three essential building blocks. Just as the food pyramid visually depicts our need for proteins, grains, fruits, and vegetables, affection also needs three nutrients in order to survive. Before we get into the specific ways to nourish your marriage, let's look at these essentials that provide a foundation for growth. An affectionate marriage needs:

- **Closeness** apparent through efforts to woo your spouse and engage him or her at both an emotional and spiritual level.
- **Tenderness** evident through kindness, thoughtfulness, and respect. My fortune cookie at lunch today said, "If you had a penny for every kind act, you'd surely be a millionaire." If only that were so in the majority of marriages today.
- **Passion** shown by expressions of spontaneous or creative physical intimacy that is focused on your mate, not on yourself.

We'll discuss each of these essentials later on in the book. You may be thinking you're the wrong one to be reading this material because your spouse is the one who isn't tender, close, or passionate. But keep reading, because I'm talking to you, the affection-starved person. Your actions, even if you're acting alone, can make a difference your spouse will notice. The changes you make in your own attitudes, behavior, and words can draw even a reluctant partner back to the banquet table.

For the first six years of their marriage, Mitch and Suzanne enjoyed all three building blocks. They longingly recalled taking long walks hand in hand, talking candidly and in detail about their dreams and goals. During those early years, Suzanne was hard at work, financially putting her husband through college, while Mitch was focused on being a successful student and mate. They played together and shared with each other. They were simply having a great time as loving partners. Not surprisingly, Suzanne refers to this period as the "good years."

Things started to change, however, by year seven. By then, they had two young children, and Mitch had finished his graduate degree in engineering. It was during this crucial, maturing stage of their marriage that Suzanne and Mitch started to slowly drift apart. She was now a working mom, dealing with all the stresses that creates, while Mitch was heavily investing his time and effort into moving up the corporate ladder. Life was good, but their love for each other wasn't. The walks stopped. The talks ended. The dreaming ceased. Expressions of tenderness became fewer and farther between, and the bond of closeness was weakening. "I didn't feel cherished by Mitch any longer," Suzanne confessed. Mitch responded, "I was doing the best I could to provide for the family, but it was never enough for her. I wanted her to stop 'feeling' and start looking at what I was doing for her and the children."

INFECTIOUS AFFECTION

It's easy for couples to slip into patterns like Suzanne and Mitch's, where work and responsibility crowd out togetherness. I pointed out that affection, or the lack thereof, is contagious. One marriage partner can "infect" the other by showing even small amounts of affection, helping the receiving spouse to show more affection as well.

It only takes a little affection over an extended period of time to infect your marriage for good.

God wants spouses to affect each other positively. In Deuteronomy 24:5 we read, "When a man has taken a new wife, he shall not go out to war or be charged with any business; he shall be free at home one year, and bring happiness to his wife whom he has taken." Isn't that an interesting verse? God says when you get married, guys, don't work for a whole year. All you are to do is spend a year making your wife happy. Wives might think he'd just be underfoot for a whole year and he should be going to work, but I think God may have said that because men are so dense that it takes a whole year to start to be able to relate to their wives. God said to concentrate on your relationship with your wife and make her happy. Find out what pleases her and what her needs are and start loving her the way she needs to be loved. That's what I mean by affecting your spouse.

You may be thinking, *I'm stretched to the limit as far as time goes*, but you can find enough time to show affection to your spouse if you try. And maybe your schedule needs some reprioritizing as well.

Affection increases the feeling of belonging in a marriage. I've seen alienated spouses blossom under affection and dispositions change from surly to sympathetic. Spouses have the power to affect each other. If I go home tonight and say, "Donna, you look terrific. Thank you for being my wife, for taking care of the house. Tell you what, why don't we just go out to dinner tonight? I just want to talk to you about your life and how things are going with you," did I affect her? Of course!

On the other hand, if I go home and say, "Oh man, the house is a mess. I thought dinner was going to be ready. Can't you get with the program?" I affected my wife negatively.

When we affect another person, we either draw her closer or push her away. We increase either her sense of belonging or her sense of aloneness. How to affect our spouse for the better is the all-important question because everybody's affected by different things. We need to figure out how to build up and encourage, rather than discourage and tear down. But almost everyone is positively affected by affection, time together, and appreciation.

GREAT EXPECTATIONS?

In a perfect world a spouse would always get it the first time, right? But in that unrealistic world I wouldn't even need to write about affection in marriage because it wouldn't be a problem.

But we don't live in a utopia, nor does anyone dwell with a flawless person. By keeping your expectations reasonably low, you lessen the chance that you will be disappointed. Remember the formula:

Expectation - reality = disappointment

By focusing on what you can be thankful for about your spouse instead of what he's *not* doing, your level of contentment will increase. Even if your spouse doesn't seem to care how to best connect with you, be on the lookout for any flicker of affection, and let him know you appreciate it and why. Express your appreciation in as specific a way as possible, like,

"Thank you for asking about my meeting today. I really appreciated your interest." Affirmation goes a long way toward thawing relationships and increasing affection.

So does easing off of high expectations and adding a dose of reality to what you can reasonably expect your spouse to do.

Of course, God can do much more than we can ask or imagine. I've seen him do it many times. Expecting God to do great things is different from expecting your spouse to be perfect, or nearly so, and that kind of expectation of God is simply the faith the Bible talks about in Hebrews 11:1 (NASB), "Now faith is the assurance of things hoped for, the conviction of things not seen."

One of the greatest gifts we can give a spouse is acceptance—acceptance of who he or she really is, without demands for his meeting our idealized expectations.

THE THREE H'S OF AFFECTION

We can affect our spouse or another person in three basic ways: with our hand, with our heart, and with our head.

The *hand* represents practical behaviors. If I help Donna, if I give her a hand, that's my way of showing affection to her. She likes that and she feels closer to me. She told me that the thing that she enjoys more than anything is just being out in the yard working together, digging up weeds, smoothing rocks. Yard work means less to me, but it makes her feel close to me. The hand represents the physical aspect of relating to another person.

The *heart* represents the emotional connection our spouse needs. I can be emotionally connected through my words—for example, "Donna, I'm sorry about that," "Tell me more about that," or "I really appreciate you"—and also through my nonverbal looks. I can influence her emotions by my facial expressions: a smile, a wink, an understanding nod.

The third H is the *head*, which represents the intellect. People grow closer to one another when they share a hobby, read together, or share in learning something new. Similar intellectual interests can create a strong connection between a husband and wife.

In our marriage relationship, we affect each other with all three: hand, heart, and head. But many of us only know how to show affection in one of these ways. I've talked to people who have intellectual marriages where it's all theoretical. They're committed, but there's no emotion. One widow told me her husband had shown love during their forty-year marriage, but she knew he did it out of obligation. It was a head thing. He did it because he was a Christian man and knew he was supposed to do these things. She appreciated it, but she said she never felt connected to him. He was great at the head area but not at the heart area.

Others try to build relationships emotionally but without ever talking about intellectual things or being involved with physical activities together. And some people just want to show love with their hands—by helping with tasks, or through sex or other physical contact.

In marriage the key is figuring out what type of connecting is most important to your spouse, through the hand, heart, or head. Then think about how often you connect each way and make a conscious decision to begin connecting in the most effective way—the way your spouse prefers. All three types of connection are necessary. The question is in what order. In many ways, I am first a head person and secondarily a hand person. One of my love languages is words of affirmation. When Donna takes the time to say, "Randy, I really appreciate what you're doing," I feel close to her because she is acknowledging my efforts. I feel good knowing she comprehends what I'm trying to do.

When we get married, we assume and expect that our spouse knows how to love us. I used to think that, but after years of working with people, I realize this is unfair because no one is a mind reader. Unless you share with your spouse how you need to be loved, he or she can't know it. I talk to guys who don't have a clue how to love their wives and to women who don't know how to love their husbands. Both of you must tell each other how to connect. When do you feel closest to your spouse? When do you share emotionally? When you're physical and you're doing physical things together, sexual or nonsexual? Or is it when you are sharing intellectually, talking with each other? Which way is more important to you? Let your spouse know this crucial information.

For example, when I show Donna how to make love to me, I'm being fair to her and to my marriage, and I'm also being good to myself. Married couples often don't talk about what we like sexually, physically, or emotionally. We wind up as two people dancing around, making guesses, wondering, and assuming. Check out your assumptions with your spouse and show what makes you feel connected.

I find that many times a spouse—more often a woman than a man—wants her husband to read her mind. Women want men to know how to love them, but in the fallen world in which we live, the distance between man and woman is like a giant wall. Without shared information, your spouse can't scale that wall and connect with you.

Laura confirmed the importance of shared information when she talked to me about her forty-year marriage to an unaffectionate husband. She said, "What I wish more than anything is that I had started right at the beginning, saying to my husband, 'If you want to make me happy this is how you have to love me.' I never would have imagined saying something like that forty years ago, but I think young women should gently teach their husbands how to love. That's something I would do if I had it to do over again, specifically tell him and show him how to hold me, how to hug me, how to make love to me. If you have a problem early on, address it, and whatever it takes, deal with it then."

Laura would have applauded the way Courtney and her husband communicated their needs to each other. Courtney said, "In the very beginning, we had an agreement that we have no idea what each other needs, so we need to tell each other. He hasn't been living with me my whole life, so there's no way for him to know what I need. So when we're in an argument or something, sometimes I'll turn around to him and I'll be like, 'You know what? What I really need is a hug.' So that's how we keep things going really smooth. We've been married four years, and we've had two major fights."

Surprised, I asked her how she got so smart. She said, "I grew up without a dad so I watched other people's marriages. The ones that succeeded were the ones where I noticed the women were really kind of telling their husbands, 'This is what I need you to do.' And it goes into all areas of our marriage. I'll tell him 'I need you to hang your coat up.' And he'll forget, but I understand that he's trying."

GOING IT ALONE/TAKING THE FIRST STEP

But what if your spouse doesn't seem to care how to connect with you? What if your efforts to share fall on deaf ears? You can still move toward that banquet table by yourself.

Try to understand your spouse's needs. Is he or she primarily a hand person, a heart person, or a head person? Once you think you know which method will connect with your spouse most effectively, make a definite effort to connect in that way.

Follow the adage "Show, don't tell." Act instead of just talking about it. If your spouse is a hand person, offer to help with a project. If she's a head person, get interested in one of her interests and learn something about it. When you share what you've learned, she'll know you're trying to connect and she will probably respond favorably. If your spouse is a heart person, express your feelings, especially positive ones. It may not make a difference the first time you do it, or the second, third, or dozenth time. But I can guarantee you that your determination to understand your spouse's needs and meet them will have an impact for the better, no matter how long it takes.

And when you get the opportunity to tell your spouse what you need and how to connect with you, by all means do it! If you don't tell your spouse what makes you feel closer, you're not being fair to your marriage.

You might be thinking, *"Why should I have to tell him what I need?"* Simply put, if you don't, your spouse may not "get it" on his own. Waiting for your partner to figure out what is missing in your marriage isn't worth the frustration or the risk.

Carrie had thoughts along these lines. When I talked to her, she had a pretty empty love tank. She said, "I have shared with my husband over the years that I do not feel significant. Because he is a man of facts and ideas and very much efficiency-oriented, I have felt that my ideas, my concerns, my values, hopes, and dreams really do not matter.

"He doesn't understand the feeling part. I think he's pretty much all head and very little heart. But I think the Lord is working on the heart part. I guess he just does not know how to relate to my heart, and that's what has been the most painful thing in our marriage. We can enjoy life together, we can play, we can solve issues. But it's that emotional intimacy that has been missing, and that has truly depleted my tank.

"It's almost as though he disconnects when we get to talking on an emotional level. I can see it in his eyes. I have, perhaps, a couple of moments to be able to interject what I need to say and then I can see it, almost like a shutdown. He's aware of it, but we're not quite sure how to remedy the situation. By gradually increasing his attention span, we've made some progress. I try to say what I'd like to say succinctly, and he tries to focus for increasing periods, just a minute or two more every evening. Since we both have the desire to improve, gradual movement in the right direction is helping us."

It was different for Denise and Greg. They had both assumed that the feelings of love would just go on forever. It's not that Greg wasn't committed to his marriage or spending time with Denise. He just became preoccupied with life and forgot to pay attention to the all-important building blocks of tenderness, closeness, and passion.

Denise admitted that she probably needs more affection than Greg is able to give. Even before they got married, Greg said he thought, *It's never going to be enough with Denise. If I'm not right there for her every time she wants to talk, I'm going to be in trouble.* But instead of dealing with this issue ahead of time, they both ignored it and assumed it would all work out somehow after the wedding day. Greg and Denise ignored the warning signs and moved forward under an illusion that everything would be all right because at that time it was. But now, well into their marriage, they both need a plan to help them experience the type of genuine affection each desires for their relationship.

A PLAN FOR PLANTING

Denise took a two-pronged approach to laying the nutritional foundation for growth in her marriage. First, she recognized that she needed to find healthy ways to meet some of her needs instead of expecting Greg to provide everything.

She realized that developing her friendships with other women would help her find an outlet for talking through the joys and challenges of motherhood and would also provide companionship. She considered becoming involved in a church activity that would help to broaden her sphere of acquaintances and take the emphasis off of her need for Greg's attention. As a working mother, her time for outside activities and friendships was limited. Denise began by scheduling a social activity for herself twice a month, even if it was just lunch with a friend. This outlet helped to ensure that some of her emotional needs would be met through appropriate relationships with others.

Second, Denise decided to show affection to her husband through "infectious affection." She decided not to wait for Greg to show her the affection she desired. Instead, she took the lead. She began with this short list of practical things she could do: (We'll talk more about several of these later in the book.)

- Ask how your spouse is doing today . . . and really listen.
- Hold your partner—without it leading to sex.
- Create "planned spontaneity." In other words, arrange ahead of time to do something special for your spouse, but make it seem spur-of-the-moment.
- Bring home an unexpected, meaningful gift uniquely suited for your spouse.

- 🐚 Set aside your own priorities in order to get something done on your partner's to-do list.
- 🐚 Know your spouse's favorite music—bring home a surprise CD and listen to it with your partner.
- 🐚 Express thoughtful words of appreciation to your mate.
- 🐚 Observe when your spouse is dressed especially nicely and make a positive comment.
- 🐚 Be interested in your partner's hobbies and outside interests.

You don't have to do *all* these things every day. In fact, to do so would probably lessen their impact. The point is when you become infectiously affectionate, you discover and routinely practice small ways to lovingly influence your marriage for a lifetime.

When Denise began practicing the infectious affection principle, Greg noticed the difference and he, too, wanted to build more affection into their marriage. He said, "I completely messed up with Denise. I knew something was bothering her, but with Denise it never seemed she was very happy—with me at least. I should have been concentrating and noticed it sooner, though." Greg is far from being alone when it comes to missing signals from a spouse. He was simply doing what many of us, especially men, do each day—*mistake routine for satisfaction.*

I wrote out an assignment for them to go home and work on over the next month. It focused on four areas:

1. *Study your spouse.* In the apostle Peter's discourse on wives and husbands in 1 Peter 3, we find the attributes of a "holy" woman: purity, reverence, a gentle and quiet spirit—all traits God can use to win over an unbelieving husband. I instructed Greg to look more closely at Denise's inner beauty and discern what it is that makes her different from any other woman on earth. "Focus on her unique gifts and talents," I told him. "Observe Denise and try to identify at least five things that set her apart from others and show her to be a godly woman."

Take some time to think about your spouse: his strengths, his goals, his likes and dislikes. Make a study of him. Make a list of his positive attributes. The more you know about him, the more you can show affection in a way he will understand and appreciate.

Put yourself in your spouse's shoes and try to fill in the blanks in the following statements. Answer as you think he or she would answer.

- I feel most respected by you when you _____.
- I feel closest to you when you _____.
- I know you love me when you _____.
- My greatest fear for the future is _____.
- The most affectionate thing you have ever done was

  _____.
- When you touch me I _____.
- What most attracted me to you was

  _____.
- My greatest desire for the future is

  _____.
- If I could change one thing about our marriage it would be _____.
- The one thing I would like to know about you is

  _____.

This exercise may have been challenging for you because you might not be sure how your spouse would complete these statements. If the opportunity presents itself, you could use these statements as conversation starters. Putting yourself in your spouse's place and trying to answer as he would will help you discover the best ways to connect.

2. Affect your spouse. I asked Denise and Greg to do one little thing each day to show affection to each other in a way the other person would recognize and appreciate. I told Denise, "At this step you need to start showing Greg how special he is to you through your words and actions and in language he will understand." This may require some out-of-the-box thinking, but it's worth it. The key is doing whatever *isn't* expected. The goal is to see the self-protective walls start to come down. A change in scenery can be good for a marriage. You might try, for example, planning a weekend away for just the two of you. Or take the initiative to find front row seats at your spouse's favorite sporting event or concert, planned around a dinner at a nice restaurant you have never tried. Or plan your spouse's favorite meal or snack and prepare it for her at home. Surprise your spouse by doing a chore you know she would like to have done for her. Often, this simple change in routine will be enough to crumble the emotional barriers and permit some serious sharing.

3. Communicate with your spouse. At this point you need to be ready with words that matter to you and make sense to your spouse. In other words, you must speak her language or she will likely miss what you're asking for. For example, if your spouse is a logical-type person, then speak from your heart with words that will speak to the head. If he or she tends to think in terms of the bottom line in life, then lovingly but firmly get straight to the point. Remember the biblical example of the apostle Paul, and how he went to great pains to communicate the gospel to the different Gentile people groups using words and illustrations they would understand. In 1 Corinthians 9:22, he says he becomes "all things to all men, that I might by all means save some." By speaking words and using illustrations his audience would understand, Paul was effective in his communication. You need to do the same thing with your spouse in order to be an effective communicator of your love.

And your communication must be specific. I like to speak with specifics, while Donna prefers to make observations. When our children were little and needed help getting to bed, Donna would say something like, "Randy, don't you think the kids ought to go to bed?" Of course I did, but I soon discovered that she wasn't looking for agreement to her observation. She wanted to see some action—more specifically, action from *me*. It was Donna's way of asking me to get up out of my recliner and put the kids to bed. "Why couldn't you just say so?" I told her then (and still tell her every now and then—with a smile). By disposition, Donna is not a demanding person. Her observations are her quiet way of pointing out what needs to be done. She's learned this way is safer and results in fewer rolled eyes and adolescent behavior—from the kids and myself.

Nevertheless, making an observation about the need for the kids to go to bed is one thing; an observation that your marriage is going down the tubes is quite another. You need more than an observation; you must use words that are descriptive, clear, heartfelt, and results-focused. You might want to try these types of phrases:

"Honey, I am very concerned about the lack of affection between us. Sometimes I feel so much distance from you that I wonder if, in fact, you aren't from Mars and I'm not from Venus, and it scares me. We really need to talk about this before it gets to be a more serious problem for our marriage."

"Sweetheart, I feel like I'm one of your employees in a staffing meeting. You tell me what needs to get done, but I don't feel like I really know you very well. I didn't marry a boss; I married you, and I need for you not to treat me like hired help."

"Yesterday, when I was so upset over the problem I'm having with Jimmy's teacher, I needed for you to understand my problem. When you said, 'You should just forget about it and get on with your life,' I really felt that you didn't care. You need to know that when you ignore my feelings it leaves me feeling pretty distant from you. A little hug and a few words of understanding would have been helpful and appreciated."

Remember, as I mentioned at the beginning of the book, sometimes nothing you can do works if you are facing issues like abuse, addiction, mental illness, or chronic adultery, in addition to being starved for affection. In chapter 8, we'll talk about what to do when nothing seems to work in situations like those. But for those of us with pretty average marriages, clear communication is a big help.

I would caution you to remember, however, that boldly speaking the truth is only half of the biblical formula: "Instead, speaking the truth *in love*, we will in all things grow up into him who is the Head, that is, Christ" (Ephesians 4:15, NIV, emphasis added). Be sure your communication is loving.

4. Focus on your spouse. I talked to Greg about 1 Peter 3:7 (NIV), "Husbands, in the same way be considerate as you live with your wives, and treat them with respect." Then I flipped the Bible back a few chapters to Ephesians 5:25 (NIV), a verse I believe should be memorized and serve as a theme for all Christian husbands: "Husbands, love your wives, just as Christ loved the church and gave himself up for her."

"Do you see where the emphasis lies?" I asked Greg. "You need to place Denise first, regardless of whether you feel you're getting anything back from her. Your love for Denise is to be unconditional and sacrificial, just like Jesus' love for you." I wanted Greg to make Denise the center of his focus.

I also asked Denise to put Greg first. We read in Ephesians 5:21 (NIV), "Submit to one another out of reverence for Christ." Making your spouse the center of your attention can only help your marriage.

THE BOTTOM LINE

You've probably noticed that what I'm suggesting is getting your attention off of yourself and onto your spouse, whether or not you think he or she deserves it. When all is said and done, we are commanded by God to *love*!

- "This is the message you heard from the beginning: We should love one another." (1 John 3:11, NIV)
- "God is love. Whoever lives in love lives in God, and God in him. In this way, love is made complete among us. . . . There is no fear in love. But perfect love drives out fear." (1 John 4:16-18, NIV)
- "In this same way, husbands ought to love their wives as their own bodies. He who loves his wife loves himself. After all, no one ever hated his own body, but he feeds and cares for it, just as Christ does the church—for we are members of his body. 'For this reason a man will leave his father and mother and be united to his wife, and the two will become one flesh.'" (Ephesians 5:28-31, NIV)

These verses show us that love is not an option for a Christian; it's a command. And the command applies even to a spouse who is not relating to you in the ways you need.

I encourage affection-starved people to give what they'd like to be getting: attention and affection. Look for points of shared interest or responsibility and build on those by talking about them and working together. Intimacy can come out of many areas besides emotional and physical affection. Couples can experience recreational intimacy, spiritual intimacy, intellectual intimacy, and many others. We'll talk about these in the remaining chapters. In fact, God's original plan included intimacy on all levels. When he said it was not good for Adam to be alone (Genesis 2:18), he wasn't referring to his need for a cook, nurse, or sex partner. What the first man needed, and what you need, is a helpmate, friend, lover, and companion. You *can* get to the abundance of that wondrous banquet table in your relationship. Your marriage can be a veritable feast where you and your spouse are both fed, nourished, and nurtured. This book can help you get there. Stay tuned!

The remainder of this book is dedicated to helping affection-starved people put together a game plan that will hopefully lead to a *breakthrough marriage*. The walls between you and your spouse have points of weakness, and I intend to help you find them so you can tear those walls down.

BUT I DON'T *FEEL* LIKE IT!

In this chapter we talked about the need to experience your feelings. But do you need to "feel" like showing affection in order to do it? The answer is no. I've found that sometimes I don't feel like forgiving another person, but if I do it out of sheer obedience to God who requires it of me, the feelings of forgiveness will eventually follow my obedience. Feelings always follow thought and behavior.

It's the same way in your marriage. You may feel anything but affectionate toward your spouse. But if you begin to act out affection, you could be surprised when your feelings catch up with your actions.

In his book *The Fine Art of Friendship*, Ted W. Engstrom tells of a man named Joe who was so upset with his wife that he decided to divorce her. But before serving her the papers, he made an appointment with a psychologist with the specific purpose of finding out how to make life as difficult as possible for her.

The psychologist said, "I've got the perfect solution. Starting tonight, treat your wife as if she were a goddess. Change your attitude 180 degrees. Start doing everything in your power to please her. Listen to her when she talks about her problems, help around the house, take her out to dinner on weekends. Then, after two months of this wonderful behavior, just pack your bags and leave her. That should get to her!"

That night Joe implemented the plan. He couldn't wait to do things for her. He brought her breakfast in bed, had flowers delivered to her for no particular reason, and took her on romantic weekends. They even read books to each other at night, and Joe listened to her as never before. He kept this up for the full two months. After the allotted time, the psychologist gave Joe a call at work. "Joe," he asked, "how's it going? Did you file for divorce? Are you a happy bachelor once again?"

"Divorce?" asked Joe. "Are you kidding? I'm married to a goddess. I've never been happier in my life!"[4]

The idea, of course, is that when he began to show love to his wife, she responded, and they fell in love all over again.

There's no guarantee that this will happen in every marriage. But if you start loving the spouse God has given you by showing affection even when you don't think it's deserved, I can guarantee your efforts will be noticed.

Only God can give you the strength to survive in a lonely or loveless relationship and reach out to your spouse even when you may not feel like it. After all, he loved us when we were pretty unlovable (Romans 5:8), and he can show you how to be loving and affectionate in your situation as well.

Chapter 8

OVERCOMING ROADBLOCKS THROUGH REALITY RESPECT[5]

I hate roadblocks. Anything that keeps me from my destination is frustrating. Recently I was late for a flight out of the Phoenix airport when I ended up on a back street that took me to a dead end where the street ran headlong into the east-west runway. There was no way I could get across to the other side and to the terminal without backing up and taking the long way around. Knowing I was going to be late for my flight, I became frustrated and decided that all the reasons I was going to be late were the fault of the city, county, or state—whoever designed and approved the street patterns.

What do you do when you hit an immovable roadblock? There are really three choices:

1. Look for another way to get to your destination.
2. Blame someone for blocking your progress. After all, it's their fault that you're stuck where you are. Keep blaming them for impeding your movement.
3. Sit and wait. Listen to the radio . . . read a book . . . relax. You won't be frustrated, but you'll never get anywhere.

The same three choices are available when you encounter a relationship roadblock where you just can't see over the hill of problems to the other side where you want to be. Personal road-blocks can last a lifetime. In fact, you may be in a relationship where all your hopes, prayers, and persuasions just aren't giving you the desired results. You thought if you said the right thing, pushed the right button, or saw the right counselor, somehow love would appear, the roadblocks in your marriage would be removed, and you would experience the kind of marital close-ness, intimacy, and affection you desire. Unfortunately, life of-ten doesn't work that way.

Relationship roadblocks can seem just as insurmountable as a barrier or blockade across the highway. How do we get be-yond those interpersonal barriers?

When faced with a relationship roadblock, we often:

- blame our spouse for not changing
- sit and wait for something to change
- gripe to our counselor or our friends about the person we're married to
- fantasize about getting out
- become manipulative in trying to change the situation
- threaten that if things don't change, we're leaving

Roadblocks are inevitable. We're warned in Scripture "that in the last days perilous times will come: For men will be lovers of themselves, lovers of money, boasters, proud, blasphemers, disobedient to parents, unthankful, unholy, unloving, unfor-giving, slanderers, without self-control, brutal, despisers of good, traitors, headstrong, haughty, lovers of pleasure rather than lovers of God, having a form of godliness but denying its power" (2 Timothy 3:1-5). That verse probably makes your spouse seem like a saint, doesn't it?

Unfortunately, roadblocks to intimacy are often the rule

rather than the exception in marriage relationships. I'd like to describe some of the more obvious roadblocks and provide you with specific help through an approach I've coined as "Reality Respect." It's not punishment or manipulation. It doesn't require the use of anger. And it's the most powerful tool I know of, next to prayer, that can have a radical positive impact on attitudes, behaviors, and relationships. And when combined with prayer, it's almost unbeatable. In fact, you'll probably recognize situations throughout this book where Reality Respect could be applied.

What needs to happen when you hit what appears to be a permanent relationship roadblock toward your goal of closeness, affection, and intimacy in your marriage?

REALITY RESPECT . . . WHAT IS IT AND WHY DOES IT WORK?

Reality Respect shows a person that we love and respect him enough to hold him accountable for his behavior with natural and logical consequences. It is a respectful response to those people who are most important to us in our life. When we respect someone, even when he doesn't appear to deserve it, we are showing the highest form of love. It's more than being kind or patient or longsuffering, all of which are appropriate forms of love. But Reality Respect also includes accountability. In other words, he doesn't get away with things simply because we love him. In fact, *because* we love him so much, we can't allow him or ourselves to get away with inappropriate behaviors or attitudes. Reality Respect is Bible-based: "Whatever a man sows, this he will also reap" (Galatians 6:7, NASB). Reality Respect is all about natural consequences of our behavior, reaping what we sow.

When we remind a spouse or child over and over about doing something she's supposed to be doing, we show that person disrespect. We're saying, in essence, "I don't think you're smart enough, good enough, wise enough, or capable enough to take care of yourself. Therefore, I've got to remind you or do it for you." Reality Respect shows a loved one that we have reasonable expectations of what she's capable of doing and as a result we hold her accountable for doing what she should. If she doesn't bother to follow through, she experiences the natural consequences of her failure to handle her responsibilities.

If a college student fails to sign up in time for the courses she wants to take, she will miss out on those classes this semester. These natural consequences will be a far better teacher than a nagging and cajoling parent.

Reality Respect allows us to keep the big picture in view. In difficult relationships, constant problems often drag us down and we lose perspective. Only with the big picture in view are we able to stay positive and develop healthy strategies. If you're to be an honoring spouse in a difficult, unloving marriage, it's important for you to be fully engaged in an understanding and use of Reality Respect.

. . . AND WHAT IS IT NOT?

Reality Respect is *not* a form of payback or manipulation. If you use sexual games like withholding sex, or communication games such as giving your spouse the "silent treatment," you're not showing the honor that God commands us to show to one another. Reality Respect always honors your spouse, your children, God, and yourself, providing a biblical model for addressing a problem—not only in marriage but in all relationships, including your relationship with your children if you are a parent.

Robin's husband, Richard, had a temper that flared in her direction often. Robin always claimed to forgive him when he apologized, but the next day she would go shopping and charge several new and expensive outfits for herself, knowing they could not afford it and that Richard disliked using credit cards except for emergencies. Robin was not employing Reality Respect. She was using manipulation and revenge to try to make her point that she disliked and was hurt by Richard's rages.

The apostle Peter said, "Honor all people. Love the brotherhood. Fear God. Honor the king" (1 Peter 2:17). Doing that can be very difficult when the person we are commanded to honor and respect shows little honor or respect to us or our marriage. But we *can* honor a difficult or unloving spouse when we show him or her Reality Respect.

BENEFITS OF REALITY RESPECT

- **It's proactive.** It eliminates the feeling of throwing up our hands and asking, *What can I do?* It's action-oriented. Instead of sitting back and waiting, Reality Respect makes something happen. Instead of trying to change your spouse (which almost never works), you allow the realities of life and God's discipline to work.
- **It gets you off the hook.** It may be that you want to stay on the hook because you're more of the problem than you'd like to honestly admit. We'll discuss that side of the equation a bit later. But for now let's focus on how Reality Respect allows you to give your spouse's problems back to her without feeling like you need to fix her, blame her, criticize her, or tell her what to do.
- **It allows your spouse to face himself.** Whenever we

get in the way of someone truly seeing himself for who he is—his attitudes, beliefs, and behaviors—we provide a way of escape or avoidance and keep him from truly understanding what needs to be changed.

▓ **It helps you lower your frustration level and reduces feelings of guilt and anger.** By putting the responsibility in its rightful place you unburden yourself from an unnecessary weight.

HOW DO I IMPLEMENT REALITY RESPECT?

First, calmly assess what is really going on. Ask God for wisdom and clarity in analyzing your situation. Commit your marriage to him and ask for his help. Prayer moves the heart of God, as I've seen in many marriages. Perhaps until now you've been struggling with rejection and pain from the lack of affection in your marriage and it's been hard to communicate or deal with your spouse. For Reality Respect to work, you need to carefully think about the source of your problem. It's imperative that you clearly describe what's happening in your relationship. This will require you to rise above your feelings and to think dispassionately about your situation.

Second, honestly look at your part in the situation. You must be honest with yourself, asking, *How have I contributed to this problem?* One of the toughest things to do is break out of denial. But in order to make progress and achieve the affectionate marriage you desire, you must be honest with yourself and ask, *Is this his problem or mine?*

We're not establishing blame or labeling either of you as the "bad person." But if you misdiagnose the problem and blame your spouse wholly for something that is largely your responsibility, nothing is going to get better. For example, a husband might get upset that his wife isn't more affectionate when they go to bed at night, but he's forgetting that he yells at her many evenings when the kids' bedtime-delaying tactics annoy him. This requires honest thinking and praying about what the problem is and coming to an understanding, hopefully together and if not, at least by yourself, as to where the problem lies. You just might find that what you've been calling "her problem" is actually "our problem" because ultimately it affects both of you, or even "my problem" because your insensitive actions have contributed to a negative response from your spouse.

As you work on being honest with yourself, spend some time in reflection, remembering that we can learn a great deal about ourselves when we go through difficult times. It's also during these times that we gain deeper understanding of what others are going through and become more sensitive and empathetic to people in need.

Ask yourself, *What am I learning about myself and my life through my relationships? What is my true source of acceptance and love—another person or God? How do I relate to others in relationships? Do I encourage them, build them up, and show them the kind of love and affection they deserve? Do I pray for myself? For my spouse? For others? Am I asking God to change other people or to change me?*

Third, develop a simple written strategy. If you're the type of person who thrives on planning, organizing, and keeping checklists, you're probably what I refer to as a *head person*, described in chapter 7. If so, this will be right up your alley. You'll love having a checklist of things to do to make your relationship better. Just be careful that you don't allow a checklist mentality to take over in such an important area of your life. While you need to develop a strategy, remember that strategies also require flexibility and understanding to be successful. Your strategy might go something like this: When my spouse doesn't feel like sitting and talking with me when he comes home from work and instead watches TV all evening, falling asleep in the recliner, I'm going to go to bed without waking him up. You might even pray for him. Intentional decisions will strengthen you and provide some relief from your affection hunger.

If, however, you're more of an intuitive person—a take-it-as-it-comes type of individual who goes by your feelings, you're what I refer to as a *heart person*. You may find the written strategy to be more of a challenge. But you can do this, and I promise you it will result in change. Initially, it may not be the change you hoped for and, in fact, it may not even move in the direction you hoped for. There are no guarantees when it comes to human relationships. But I can assure you that as you change your response to the problems in your marriage by using large and consistent doses of Reality Respect, something will happen, something that will, in the long run, move you closer to the affectionate marriage you desire.

THREE KEYS TO SUCCESS USING REALITY RESPECT

Key #1: Focus only on present behavior and attitudes. If you've been dealing with issues from the past that never seem to get resolved, it would be best to get those on the table and settled first. Unless you take care of unresolved issues from the past, they will show up in present day behaviors and attitudes. It's important to confess and forgive the past, move on to the present, and stay there. Yesterday can't be undone, but today and tomorrow can be better. A behavior or attitude that is right in front of you today—untruthfulness, disrespect, or lack of physical affection—that's something that *can* be addressed and dealt with successfully. Once you have settled past issues, resolve to never bring them up again, because doing so would only be destructive.

Key #2: Clearly express your needs, desires, and wants. This must be done with respect and in a way your spouse can understand. I would caution you, however, to remember that *Expectations - Reality = Disappointment.* Don't set yourself and your spouse up for failure by being unrealistic or vague. You need to be specific and loving, both of which may prove difficult because of past hurts. Consider your spouse's situation as well. Perhaps he is deficient in some life experiences: He may not have received much affection as a child, or maybe she's going through a particularly difficult professional or personal problem. Take these things into account as you determine what is realistic in your relationship.

As you talk to your spouse about what you need, don't get distracted by other topics that can drag you away from the current issue. It's easy to get sidetracked in your communication and allow frustration, anger, resentment, and inertia to get you stuck.

You may be thinking, *Why should I have to tell my spouse how to love me?* As we've seen earlier, it's important to take the responsibility to help train your spouse how to love you in the way that you need to be loved, without expecting him or her to read your mind.

Key #3: Keep the ball on your spouse's side of the net. Each player in a game of tennis keeps hitting the ball back to his opponent. Then it's up to the opponent to return the ball. When we say, "The ball is in your court," we mean it's the other person's turn to take action—like returning a phone call. By keeping the ball on your spouse's side of the court you stop doing what is his responsibility, covering for him, or enabling him to continue the behavior that is harming your marriage. While marriage is not a win-lose relationship and we never rejoice when our spouse drops or misses the ball, through Reality Respect we're able to hold him or her accountable. In fact, if she does fail and drop the ball, we shouldn't gloat or be happy. We celebrate her successes with her and mourn her losses with her. When she sets a goal to exercise three times a week and achieves this goal for six months, we commend her efforts with a congratulations card. When she loses a job because her company downsizes, we sympathize and offer support.

TACKLING THE TOUGH ISSUES

Let's look at some specific problem areas in many marriages and how the principles of Reality Respect can be practically applied.

Irresponsibility or laziness

If you're married to an irresponsible person, he or she needs a good dose of Reality Respect. This, more than anything, will wake her up to the importance of her responsibility in your marriage. Using the principles we've already talked about, here are some specific steps to take.

If your spouse is lazy and is not even willing to work on the problem, first seek medical advice to determine whether physical problems or a biochemical condition such as depression could be the cause. If not, move on to Key #1.

Apply Key #1 and focus on present behavior and attitudes. Be careful not to cover up for your spouse and provide an unhealthy hiding place for his or her irresponsibility. Clearly and lovingly state your concerns. Then stop nagging, which is disrespectful and nonbiblical. Make a commitment out loud to your spouse and to yourself that nagging is going to stop. Take responsibility and apologize if you've been a nagger and commit to backing off because you respect and want to honor your spouse. I can promise you that this alone will change the dynamic in your relationship.

Apply Key #2 and clearly express your needs, wants, and desires with respect and in a way your spouse is able to understand. Don't let your expectations exceed reality and create disappointment. For example, if your spouse acts irresponsibly and consistently fails to return phone calls from extended family members, you might say, "Your mother called twice last week and left messages for you on the answering machine, which I mentioned to you both times. After the second call, I called her back because I thought she should hear from us, and she again asked to speak with you but you were at work. In the future, I'd like you to call her back within two days of her calls so she doesn't worry about you."

In Galatians 6:1, we read that if a brother is caught in a sin, be careful if you restore him that you don't fall yourself. This is not a prideful activity where you're judging your spouse. It's a decision that you're in this together and you're going to change your behavior, clearly express your needs, and expect your spouse to meet them. Then you back off without nagging and hold him or her accountable.

Apply Key #3 and keep the ball on your spouse's side of the net. Let him wrestle with the realities of his irresponsibility. While you can't allow bills to go unpaid or children undisciplined or unfed, you can back off and allow your spouse's irresponsible attitudes and behaviors toward the family or your marriage to catch up with him. If your spouse is unemployed and you have been going through the Sunday newspaper and cutting out job ads, writing letters of application, and mailing his resume out for him while he relaxes in front of the TV, just stop. You may need to get a job yourself and let your husband handle child care and meals, but it's his responsibility to go out and get himself a job. When you're gone all day and he's trying to juggle everything you do at home, he may decide to get going and get employed.

Sometimes a woman feels unloved because her husband is unwilling to help out around the house with even the simplest of chores. She's tried nagging and yelling and pouting and withholding sex and everything she can think of to no avail. By employing Reality Respect she says, "Because I respect you, I can expect that you're capable of helping out and if you choose not to, a couple of logical consequences will result. For instance, some of the chores on my list won't get done, like getting the meals ready. Or I might need to use money from the family budget to hire someone to get some projects done around the house." Reality Respect simply accepts time limitations on getting everything done. One person can carry the load only so far by herself.

Emotional irresponsibility, where one spouse is unresponsive or disrespectful, also has consequences because a spouse feels less responsive to someone who is cold or rude than to someone warm and affectionate.

Use your creativity and perhaps outside help to think of logical and natural consequences that can be used to respectfully hold your spouse accountable. What you're saying is, "I love you, honor you, and respect you enough to allow you to face the consequences of your decisions."

Remember that Reality Respect isn't punishment or manipulation. If it's either of those, it's not biblical.

Addictions

Addictions of any sort undermine your marriage and detract from intimacy, affection, and love. Not only will an addiction destroy the addict's life, but also it has the potential to destroy the lives of those around her. Broken promises to quit undermine the trust that is key to a successful, affectionate marriage. You can best show respect to an addicted person you love by holding her accountable for her actions and attitudes.

Apply Key #1 and focus on present behavior and attitudes. Keep your attention on the addictive behaviors and their results on your family. Refuse to cover up for the addict's missed days of work or other natural consequences of his addiction. Ask him to get counseling or join a group that deals with addictions.

Apply Key #2 and clearly express your needs, wants, and desires. Communicate to your spouse—and this may need to come in the form of an intervention or in counseling—"I need you to be sober" or "I desire for us to be closer but your addiction is getting in the way." There is power in the clear expression of a problem. Staying vague or general is not satisfactory.

Apply Key #3 and keep the ball on your spouse's side of the net. Accountability is mandatory when a person is an alcoholic, a workaholic, a sexaholic, or is enslaved by any other addiction. In addition to expressing your needs, wants, and desires, there must be respectful consequences for this type of behavior. It may mean treatment in a health-care facility. Once again, the goal is not to manipulate or nag but to respect the person by believing he is capable of changing and expecting him to do so for the benefit of the marriage.

Abuse or control

Mistreatment makes it hard to feel affectionate because the abused person never knows when an angry or violent outburst is going to occur. Again, trust is eroded, and with it, the feelings of closeness that affection involves also begin to disappear. In dealing with abuse or control, the cycle of mistreatment and apology must stop. The abuser can't keep asking, and you can't keep granting just one more chance.

Apply Key #1 and focus on present behavior and attitudes. The present behavior is something you can't live with and must temporarily separate yourself and your children from with the help of a counselor, your pastor, or a crisis intervention center. Included in this behavior is physical violence of any kind toward you or your children and verbal, emotional, and psychological threats and control. For example, your spouse could tell you he'll divorce you and take your children away from you if you don't stop taking a class at your community college.

Apply Key #2 and clearly express your needs, wants, and desires. Once you have a plan for safety, communicate to your spouse that you will no longer permit his mistreatment of you or your children.

Apply Key #3 and keep the ball on your spouse's side of the net. Of utmost importance in cases of abuse is following through on statements about the consequences of the abuser's actions. Threatening to take action or to leave may serve to embolden the mistreatment if he knows you don't mean what you say.

Unfaithfulness
As we have said before, without trust, affection is unlikely. And as with addictions or abuse, unfaithfulness also destroys trust. While many couples have experienced repentance, forgiveness, and restoration after adultery, chronic unfaithfulness cannot be tolerated in marriage.

Apply Key #1 and focus on present behavior and attitudes. The present behavior is something you can't tolerate and must be stopped immediately. It's not enough to promise to stop a sexual relationship but continue to occasionally talk on the phone or have lunch with the person. Nor is it acceptable to promise to stop seeing him after one more good-bye date. Sometimes it is even necessary to change jobs in order to sever ties completely.

Apply Key #2 and clearly express your needs, wants, and desires. By insisting that your spouse completely break off the adulterous relationship, you make it clear that you will not live with unfaithfulness. If possible, sit down together and tell him how deeply the situation has hurt you and how you long to be reconciled if the affair stops. Also tell him that you will undoubtedly need some time to process what has happened before trust can be restored. Talk to a counselor or your pastor about following through on your refusal to stay in an adulterous marriage, whether that includes separation, intervention, or counseling.

Apply Key #3 and keep the ball on your spouse's side of the net. If your spouse makes excuses or blames you for not being affectionate enough and causing his unfaithfulness, bring him back to the consequences of his choices by following through on the results you have stated. True repentance involves taking responsibility for your choices, not feeling sorry for yourself and creating excuses as to why the affair occurred. It also involves listening to the pain of the wronged person and being willing to prove your commitment to stop the affair and give enough time for restoration to occur. False repentance, on the other hand, shifts the blame to the spouse or the person he had the affair with. It demands that trust be immediately restored once an apology is given, and it hints of self-pity on the part of the unfaithful spouse. True repentance is genuine sorrow, while false repentance is an attempt to avoid the consequences of wrongdoing.

BUT WHAT IF *I* NEED REALITY RESPECT?

Let's be honest. Many times we see the splinter in our spouse's eye and miss the log in our own. You may be facing some personal roadblocks, and Reality Respect may be just what you need to apply in your own life, after asking God to help you overcome these problems. You can respect yourself and your capacity to change by being willing to hold yourself accountable. Some of the personal roadblocks that can be helped with Reality Respect are:

- **Childhood trauma.** Look honestly at your current behavior to see how the past might be influencing your present. Hold yourself accountable to go through the process of identifying, grieving, forgiving, and healing from traumatic events in your past. Show respect for yourself by not slipping back into denial that it ever happened or into easy forgiveness where you minimize what was done. Express your needs by writing down your reasons for wanting to move beyond the hurt and pain. Keep the ball in your court by following through with counseling and treatment to deal with the problem and its impact on your life. And take responsibility for your own change and growth that will improve both your life and your marriage.
- **Lack of attraction to your spouse.** This is a difficult issue because attraction is a personal response that seems almost beyond our control. We'll talk more

about this in chapter 16, "Starved for Contentment."
I've talked to people who weren't attracted to their future spouse when they got married and yet they chose
to marry. Others have lost that feeling of attraction
over the years. But we all have a responsibility in marriage not only to *be* attractive for our spouse by taking
care of ourselves, but also to work at *being* attracted to
our spouse. It's easy to focus on the flaws and what we
don't like instead of focusing on the things we do like
and appreciate. If you're finding that you're not as attracted to your spouse as you should be, it would be
helpful to focus on current behavior or characteristics
you appreciate and express those things often. Express
your needs to be attracted to your spouse by journaling,
and especially list traits you appreciate in him or her.
Philippians 4:8 tells us what to set our minds on: what
is honorable, right, pure, lovely, of good repute, excellent, and worthy of praise. By developing thankfulness
for the good traits of our spouse, we keep the ball in our
own court by taking responsibility to appreciate our
spouse and express affection to her. Acting affectionate
and focusing on our spouse's positive traits can help us
move back toward that attraction we once felt.

🪺 **Tendency to control.** If you are a take-charge person
who gets things done, you may be successful at work
but cause havoc at home when you try to control your
family members. If you tend to be a controller, the first
step is to look honestly at your current behavior and
admit to yourself that you try to have your own way
most of the time. Then admit this to your family and
ask them for their support as you try to change. Express
your need to accomplish and achieve and also your

need to ease up at home. Keep the ball in your court by monitoring your behavior and being quick to apologize when you catch yourself in your controlling mode.

STAYING THE COURSE

Reality Respect is a model to follow in any difficult relationship, including those that are affection starved. We've looked at what Reality Respect is and how it works. We've examined the keys to success in applying Reality Respect, and we've gotten specific about how to do that in problem areas.

It's important to remember that this is not a game; it's not revenge or manipulation. It's a loving act done with respect and proper motives to improve our marriage. And it needs to be applied consistently and patiently because change doesn't happen after one week of applying the principles, and sometimes not even after a long period.

Even if you don't see the changes you so deeply desire, you will have the peace of mind and satisfaction of knowing that you are doing everything in your power to help your spouse and your marriage. You will be acting with honor and respect and in obedience to God. And you will be finished with nagging. Please don't give up, because you never know when your new and consistent approach might reach your spouse and cause the improvements you hope for.

Reality Respect is a strategy that is biblically right and has the highest probability of producing a healthy marriage. It is a lifestyle rather than an activity; you're working on a relationship, rather than a project. We all encounter relationship roadblocks from time to time and I've suggested using Reality Respect to overcome them. If we try to get around the roadblock by using the principles of Reality Respect as a club on our spouse, it may work temporarily but not long-term. This is the lowest use of the concept and should really be called manipulation.

Or we can try to get through the roadblock by using Reality Respect to hold our spouse accountable, along with encouragement, support, love, understanding, and patience. This approach will bring us closer to our goal of a satisfying and vibrant relationship. But if we apply Reality Respect not just to our spouse but also to ourselves, admitting when we're wrong and taking personal responsibility for our actions and attitudes, we reach the highest form of love. That's when we soar right over that roadblock by putting love into action.

My prayer for those who are struggling in their relationships is that you would stay focused on what truly matters and pray for your spouse and your marriage.

> Lord, I ask you to help me during times of difficulty in my relationships to remember . . .
>
> . . . that being the right person is more important than being right;
>
> . . . that having a relationship with another human being is a precious gift to be handled with care;
>
> . . . that the greatest thing I can give to another person is the gift of myself—even with all of my frailty and hurt;
>
> . . . that true forgiveness and reconciliation begins with me, and will spring from a humble spirit and a contrite heart;
>
> . . . that after I have given all I can to reconcile a broken relationship, I must trust you with the outcome and refuse to react bitterly or vengefully if I have to let that relationship go.

Lord, remind me again, and often, that at the end of my days here on earth, my success in relationships will not be measured by the number I had—but by the quality of those I still have.

It's tragic that statistics on divorce among Christians are nearly identical to the numbers pertaining to those who aren't believers. We have failed to defend marriage and make Christian marriage different and successful. While we can't individually change the state of Christian marriage on a grand scale, we can change the way things are within the four walls of our home. We can bear testimony to a hurting world that knowing Christ does indeed make a difference. As Paul writes in Colossians 3:14, "But above all these things put on love, which is the bond of perfection."

Let's turn now to some of the specific areas where affection starvation is felt. You may feel starved for closeness, tenderness, nonsexual affection, passion, shared vision, spiritual affection, trust, and/or contentment. Let's figure out together how to provide healthy nourishment to our marriage in these key areas.

Chapter 9

STARVED FOR CLOSENESS

I couldn't help but eavesdrop on the conversation of the large family sitting across from Donna and me at the food court in the shopping mall. Not that it was doing me any good, because I couldn't understand them.

We live in a culturally diverse community where about one-third of the population is from a Mexican-American heritage. As I listened to the lively discussion among members of this Hispanic family, I was at a loss. Since I had never learned Spanish, I couldn't understand a word they were saying, except for the occasional *si* or *uno*.

It was obvious that the family was excited about something. Their laughter and animated gestures drew me in and made me wish I knew what they were so happy about. After several painstaking minutes of trying to interpret the family's conversation, I was downright frustrated. What made obvious sense to them was, unfortunately, nonsense to me. I soothed myself by turning my focus to something I could more readily understand—my sandwich.

THE LANGUAGE OF CLOSENESS

Communication in marriage is not unlike my experience at the mall. Just as I was listening to the family talk but couldn't understand them, I can also hear Donna speak to me without getting her message. Sometimes she'll try to communicate with words, other times with her emotions. But unless I've learned to understand the language she's speaking—her language of closeness—I'm not going to hear her. The same rule applies to my wife: Donna needs to understand what communicates closeness to me.

As a marriage and family therapist, I've discovered that buried under layers of hurt, frustration, and loneliness is the core need of both men and women, a need that has not changed since Adam and Eve—the need to be *close*. The basic desire for closeness is universal, regardless of age or life experience. Closeness involves feeling needed, respected, cared for, and understood. Simply put, women want to feel loved by their husbands, and men want to be loved by their wives. Closeness is vital to a successful, maturing marriage.

But here's the rub. While the need is the same for both partners, the path toward having that need fulfilled is vastly different, so much so that many couples find themselves on the road to divorce because they fail to identify their spouse's language of closeness.

If you are starved for closeness in your marriage, it is likely that you and your spouse aren't speaking the same language. In this chapter, we will look at various languages spouses use and understand, enabling you to better understand your spouse's language and how it differs from your own. This understanding will enable you to create the closeness you crave by communicating in a way your spouse understands.

AFFECTIONATELY SPEAKING

What speaks closeness to a woman? According to a study by Dr. Willard Harley, the nationally acclaimed psychologist and author of *His Needs, Her Needs*, it's affection.[6] And sorry, guys . . . as unbelievable as it may seem to you, sexual foreplay, intercourse, and orgasm didn't even make the list.

Why affection? Because women feel closer to their husbands when they are capable of providing the kind of warmth and tenderness their wives need. And while affection can be communicated beneath the sheets, women typically equate the affection they desire most with nonsexual behaviors. Here's what women have told me when I've asked them to define affection:

- "When he holds me, kisses me, and tells me how wonderful I am—but stops there with no expectation for more (sex)."
- "I feel affection from his words of appreciation."
- "When he remembers what used to make us feel close when we were dating, then I feel affection."
- "Communication, openness with each other—being one in marriage and not separate."
- "When he helps out around the house without being asked."
- "Affection is when we go for long walks and he talks about what's important to him."

These women, and hundreds of others I've spoken to, express one overriding main theme: "My husband shows affection when he knows my needs and meets them and communicates his needs to me. It makes me feel close to him."

Then if she desires sexual intimacy, you're ready. If she needs a word of encouragement, you're there for her. If she wants a helping hand, you've got one for her. When the discerning man learns to speak his wife's language of affection he is, in essence, *making love* to her, all the time—just the way *she* wants it.

When Donna and I were dating, we did a lot of fun things and simply enjoyed being together. If you were to ask Donna what it was that attracted her to me back then, she would say something like, "Randy was stable and mature. I could count on him." If you pushed a little further, she'd probably throw in something about my sense of humor and good looks (at least I would like to think so).

But today, after thirty-plus years of living with Mr. Stable, things can get, well . . . a bit boring for Donna. So to guard against my natural inclination toward monotony, I've learned that it's my job to keep the fun and surprise alive in our relationship. I call it "planned spontaneity," and it works. Notice I used the word *job*. That's what it is for me. I'm the type of person who never tires of the same routine, so I have to literally *schedule* a little excitement into my marriage—the unexpected evening out, the weekend getaway from the kids, the late-night trip to the ice cream parlor, the card hidden in her lunch. If I don't plan it, it'll never happen.

Most importantly, this effort communicates affection to Donna in a way she hears loud and clear. She knows I need her and still treasure my time with her. It makes her feel *close* to me.

LET'S GET PHYSICAL

And what speaks closeness for a man? When I ask men to define what affection is for them, they usually break into a mischievous smile. After mumbling something (usually nonsensical) about communication and respect, they get around to spelling out what's really on their mind—S-E-X!

Now, that's not a bad thing. After all, men characteristically think of affection in physical terms, and are best at expressing affection to their wife in physical ways. But because it's often difficult for men to throttle back their sexual engine, they go into overdrive far too often. For many men, intercourse and orgasm are viewed as the ultimate form of closeness with their wife, and the only language of intimacy they know how to speak, at the expense of everything else.

Bob and Marie had both been married before, so they knew what they were getting into when their wedding day arrived. They enjoyed the pomp and circumstance of the ceremony, and because they had decided to wait until they were married to have sex, the honeymoon was highly anticipated. Predictably, Bob shifted straight to overdrive during their first sexual encounter, and later said the experience was "good, but not great." Marie was even less kind with her opinion.

But that wasn't the worst of it. After they made love, Bob reclined on the bed. As he savored the moment, his mind drifted to another of his passions, the L.A. Lakers. The wedding coincided with the playoffs, and he was curious as to the final score of the big game completed earlier that evening. Did Shaq and Kobe get the job done and finish off the Blazers? He didn't need to watch all the post-game analysis and interviews. He just wanted to know the *score* . . . that was all. A couple of seconds of TV, and he'd be done. So he flipped on ESPN.

It's almost a shame the cameras weren't there to capture what happened next. It would have certainly made Sportscenter's "Top Ten Plays." When Marie heard the tube come on from inside the bathroom, she made a fast break into the bedroom that would have made Kobe marvel. And the slam dunk she administered to Bob was nothing short of Shaq-tacular! Bob, no doubt, felt it for weeks.

All joking aside, Bob's grievous lack of judgment was the result of an even greater problem. Bob had no clue what made Marie feel close, even during what was supposed to be one of the most intimate and memorable moments of their relationship. Once the sex was over, everything was fine for him. He'd achieved *his* closeness with Marie, so he instantly disconnected with her. This left Marie immediately turned off, hurt, and angry. Marie later said that, at that instant, she even wondered if she had made a mistake marrying Bob.

Is this the way it's going to be? she wondered. The feeling of physical and emotional closeness she had just experienced with Bob had suddenly dropped through the floor and landed in the basement three stories down like a load of bricks. Marie couldn't imagine how this man, who minutes earlier had been so aroused, could so quickly move on to something as trivial as sports.

Bob, on the other hand, still defended his actions. He didn't understand why it was such a big deal to steal thirty seconds from his honeymoon to check out ESPN. He quipped, "It was as though I had gone out and had an affair!"

IT'S ALL IN THE FULFILLMENT

In a sense, that's exactly what Bob did, at least to Marie. She felt unappreciated and used, as if she were just there for his pleasure and nothing more. Even more, Bob had betrayed her emotionally, cutting her off mentally at a time she was most vulnerable to him. But before you make Bob the villain (after all, just because he was *insensitive* doesn't mean he was an inherent louse) and think guys are just dumb, sex-crazed animals, let's look further at how men typically view closeness.

In his study on affection, Dr. Harley discovered that what men most desire in their marriage is not just sex, but sexual *ful-*

fillment. That's why men will often report that they feel most close to their wives at the very point of ejaculation. Dr. Harley reminds us that men desire deep sexual *fulfillment,* not just great sex. All the dreams he would wish to share with her, all his feelings of security, all of his sense of rightness with the relationship—all these are captured for him in that one orgasmic moment. That may not seem terribly fair, ladies, but if you were to peer into the mind of your husband, you would discover that sexual fulfillment for him generally represents six things:

1. His way of making up with you
2. His way of being tender with you
3. His way to converse with you
4. His way of being intimate with you
5. His way of saying, "I love you"
6. In short, his way of being close to you

In fact, when I ask men to put into words what sex fulfillment means to *them* they respond:

- Sexual fulfillment makes me feel close to my wife
- Sexual fulfillment pushes problems out of my mind for a while
- Sexual fulfillment puts life back into perspective
- Sexual fulfillment makes me feel needed

One insightful woman summed it up the best when she told me, "Sex to my husband is safety, conversation, closeness, oneness, intimacy, and affection all wrapped up into one package. After we have sex, he thinks everything is okay again."

That said, men still do not have an excuse for focusing solely on sexual fulfillment. The smart man understands the reward and responsibility of his powerful sexual desires and chooses wisely. He knows that the exercise of his sexuality requires him to have self-discipline and consideration for his wife. He also realizes he must learn to speak the language of affection to his wife in a way she will understand and appreciate. One insightful man told me, "Randy, I've learned that if I want a satisfying sexual relationship with my wife, I need to be affectionate with her outside the bedroom. When something is wrong with our physical relationship, I first take a look at what *I* am doing." As a man consistently follows this good advice, he learns a wonderful truth—that an emotionally satisfied wife produces a sexually satisfied husband. In both cases *closeness* is the outcome.

SPEAKING MY LANGUAGE

Both men and women want closeness. But the paths to get there are vastly different. For a woman, closeness comes as a result of affection expressed without sex. For a man, closeness results from physical affection, achieved through sexual fulfillment.

You and your spouse want the *same thing,* despite your past experiences or personal biases. Yes, he sometimes may act like a jerk. Sure, she may seem insensitive at times. Your spouse may seem totally oblivious to your needs. But you both desire to be closer. Intimacy occurs in a relationship when the man and woman practice speaking the closeness language of their partner, whether it be verbal or nonverbal, physical or nonphysical, emotional or non-emotional.

The most accurate measure of a marriage that will endure is a couple's closeness. The *closer* you are the stronger you will become. Below are ten statements, five for the men and five for the women, that you can use as a closeness barometer. There are separate questions for men and women because each gender tends to feel close to their spouse for different reasons.

Respond to each statement below with a number between 1 and 10. A "1" means that for you that statement is not at all true of your marriage, while a "10" means that for you that statement is extremely true of your marriage. Your answers will likely be somewhere in between.

Again, answer for yourself and then answer the other set of statements as you believe your spouse would respond to them. Focus on the areas where you think he or she would give low scores to see where you might communicate closeness to your spouse in a more effective way.

WOMEN ONLY:

Our marital communication is very good._____
My husband generally anticipates and meets my needs.
_____
My husband takes time to get into my world._____
I get plenty of affection from my husband._____
I feel my husband's support._____

MEN ONLY:

I am sexually satisfied by my wife._____
I feel respected by my wife._____
I really enjoy doing things with my wife._____
I feel comfortable sharing my dreams and fears with my wife._____
I know my wife is in "my corner."_____

The ten statements above not only represent how you feel toward your spouse; they're key to understanding your spouse's language of closeness, because where low scores appear, there is room for improvement. If your spouse is willing to take part in this exercise, you can use it as a discussion starter. If you can talk about these areas and where each of you would like to do better, you'll find new ways to speak one another's language of closeness.

You can become as close in your marriage as you choose to be. If you were to set a goal to improve your spouse's responses by 20 percent, you would discover a huge improvement in the quality of your marriage and in your interpretation of your partner's closeness language.

As you learn to interpret your partner's closeness language and change your actions and attitudes to respond to that language, you will create a bond of love that will last a lifetime.

Chapter 10

STARVED FOR TENDERNESS

In an effort to reduce the amount of conflict in one small Belgian village, its mayor created a Department of Tenderness, hoping that a little more caressing, cuddling, and kissing would make everybody a bit nicer and reduce the problems in his little village.

Here in the United States, we have departments of Defense, Education, Treasury, Health and Human Services, and so on. I wonder what would be different in our country if we added a Department of Tenderness to the president's cabinet? While all families could benefit from an increased dose of tenderness, no government department or law will make it happen. It's got to be an inside job between the people who love one another enough to learn how to show tenderness.

If you are starved for tenderness in your marriage, start by becoming your family's Department of Tenderness, the one who takes the lead in being tender. Your example will probably result in your tenderness being returned. Let's see how.

WHAT IS TENDERNESS?

According to the Merriam-Webster Dictionary, *tenderness* is "having a soft or yielding texture: easily broken, cut, or damaged." Being tender exposes us to being hurt, cut, or damaged in some way. The fact is that when we're tender with our spouse or another person, he may take advantage of our vulnerability. But it's well worth it to be tender and vulnerable instead of tough and hard. Being tender is a willingness to be flexible and open; it doesn't mean being a wimp or a doormat. Tenderness requires four elements: physical touching, emotional touching, timing, and consistency.

Tenderness involves appropriate physical contact

First, I want to make the all-important distinction between what is appropriate and what is inappropriate touching. Obviously, what is appropriate in marriage would not be appropriate in a work setting. Because of the many abuses of both children and adults in the area of physical contact, some professions limit physical contact, a sensible measure. But the fear and mistrust that make even a simple pat on the arm scary are sad indeed. Many teachers and other professionals hesitate to engage in even normal, simple physical contact for fear of being accused of sexual harassment or abuse. This fear contributes to the lack of appropriate physical contact between people today.

In marriage, tenderness can and should be expressed by physical touching unless there is a medical or other reason preventing it. Skin is the largest sense organ of the body. While our eyes are our windows to the world, it's our skin that, when touched, becomes the window to our heart. Many abused people say it wasn't the physical battering that hurt them as much as the emotional damage caused by that battering. Tender touching goes a long way to heal hurts of the past and present.

Jesus often touched those he healed. He took hold of the man he healed in Luke 14:4 and he took the hand of the girl he raised from the dead in Luke 8:54. He could have healed them without touching them, as he did with the centurion's servant who was at the centurion's house some distance from Jesus. Touch was important to Jesus. When the sick woman in Luke 8:43-44 touched the hem of his garment, he knew it immediately, and he responded to her.

When a spouse is hurting, a physical touch instantly connects us and can break down barriers. Hugging, cuddling, and holding each other are very positive actions.

Tenderness involves emotional touching

If we take physical touching and multiply it by emotional touching, we see a powerful result. Physical affection is good and emotional touching is too, but combined, they can provide tremendous benefits. Emotional touching is connecting with another person at a deep level. It says, "I accept you as you are right now." An emotional touch might be a kind or understanding comment or a word of affirmation spoken to your spouse to show that you resonate with what she's going through and you understand. But touching someone appropriately while saying something insensitive undoes the benefit of the touch. Tenderness needs appropriate physical contact multiplied by an emotional touch in order to work and connect two people.

Tenderness involves timing

Timing is everything in life. If you have the right physical touch times the right emotional touch but you do it at the wrong time, it can be disastrous. When is the right time for tenderness?

- When someone you love is hurting
- When someone you love is sad

- When someone you love is discouraged
- When someone you love is confused
- When someone you love is lonely
- When someone you love has accomplished a goal
- When someone you love is celebrating an important milestone
- When someone you love is happy about a recent development in his life

The right time for tenderness is almost any time *except* . . .

- When someone you love is **angry**

When you try to be tender with an angry person, it can be perceived as being patronizing. An angry person needs understanding and, in some cases, a sense of security, safety, and strength on your part. If the anger is being demonstrated to intimidate you, tenderness is clearly not the appropriate response. You may need to leave the scene. You may need to be strong, and you may need to listen, but you probably shouldn't try to be tender.

- When someone you love is **abusive** to you

If your spouse is violent, it's not the time for tenderness. Being tender in such a situation can empower the person by giving the wrong message: that you accept him as he is now.

It's very important to understand that tenderness is a way of accepting, connecting, and loving a person where she is. In cases of very destructive behavior, such as out-of-control anger, abuse, or other violence, you need to show tough love, not tenderness.

■ When someone you love is **abusive to self**

Again, if a loved one is involved with drugs, alcohol, pornography, gambling, or any other addictive behavior, this is not a time to be tender. You can talk tenderly to her and try to understand her pain, but you must not enable the destructive behavior.

Tenderness requires consistency

Tenderness now and then isn't good enough. We need regular doses of tenderness over an extended period of time. It's better to show tenderness throughout the day in small amounts than to give large doses of tenderness occasionally.

A smile, an arm around someone's shoulders, or a hand held even for a few minutes speaks volumes of tenderness. A kind word of encouragement takes only a few seconds. Concentrated listening is another way to show care and tenderness. The idea is to express tenderness frequently and consistently. You don't want your spouse to be shocked when you smile tenderly at him, wondering what has gotten into you. The goal is to build trust so that your spouse can trust you and count on you to be tender. She needs to know that she can turn to you at the end of a bad day. If tenderness is inconsistent, your spouse will always feel she must weigh your mood before sharing problems with you.

When one or more of these four important ingredients is missing, the formula doesn't work, and the outcome is diminished greatly. Did you notice that I used multiplication instead of addition in my formula? Tenderness that is appropriately physical, emotional, timed right, and consistent multiplies exponentially, creating a positive impact for our marriage.

The benefits of tenderness

Tenderness is the main ingredient in a satisfying marriage because it is the soil in which affection can flourish and grow. Without tenderness, affection is blighted. Through tenderness, communication improves, conflicts become easier to resolve, and tension decreases. It sounds like a miracle drug, and in a sense it really is—like a powerful daily vitamin that works quietly over an extended period of time to build up your marriage and your other relationships.

A great thing about tenderness is that showing it requires very little effort. Tenderness doesn't cost any money, it takes very little time, and it doesn't require advance planning. While planned spontaneity is important, too, unplanned acts of tenderness are an important part of creating an atmosphere where affection can grow and flourish. Tenderness is positive, supportive, and one of the most intimate nonsexual things you can do. Another benefit of tenderness is that it is a direct path to deeper connection beyond the superficial. We talked earlier about our need as humans to belong, which drives us from birth until death. The meaning we search for is generally in the context of being connected with people.

As with so many other good things in life and in marriage, God designed tenderness as a part of healthy human relationships. We read in 1 Peter 3:8, "Finally, all of you be of one mind, having compassion for one another; love as brothers, be tenderhearted, be courteous." Tenderness fosters connection with others. A simple touch on the face, a hug, or a tender word can tell someone you love that he is valuable and important to you. He belongs.

Tenderness makes us feel cared for. A person may be amply provided for physically and financially, but that alone doesn't make her feel loved. We've been unusually blessed here in

America with prosperity and affluence. Most of us would be considered rich compared with the rest of the world. But even with all of this, if tenderness is missing, we will still feel that something is lacking: affection.

IN SHORT SUPPLY

Most of us intuitively know that tenderness feels good. We like to receive it and we realize it should be abundant in marriage and the family. But tenderness can be hard to give and awkward to receive. Let's look at a few factors that make tenderness scarce in many families.

We are not taught to be tender.
Tenderness is a learned response, something we choose to do. As children, most of us were taught the exact opposite—how to compete, how to protect ourselves, how to succeed in the cut-throat world and bounce back when life knocks us down—not how to be tender.

When I was growing up in Detroit in the fifties and sixties, the guys in the neighborhood often had a Saturday afternoon pickup football game in the open lot down the street. I can assure you that there was no tenderness in picking sides for that team. Whoever was the biggest and best got picked first, and the runts went last. I can never recall anyone saying, "Oh, I feel so sorry for you that you didn't get picked. I hope I didn't hurt your feelings." More likely, you would hear something like, "You mean I've got to have Bill on my team? You can have Bill. I'll take Brent."

Getting tackled and ripping open a knee became more a badge of pride than pain. I never recall any of my friends offer-ing me a Band-Aid or a hand to get up or a word or touch of encouragement. Instead, we got right back at the game, ready to pummel our opponents. That's what little boys, and now even little girls, learn in our culture.

I was blessed to grow up in a loving, supportive home, but as in most American homes, we weren't overly tender to each other. Of course, we had our times of hugs and kisses, but like most families, things were usually so hectic that taking time for those deeply expressed moments of tenderness wasn't the norm.

I'm the youngest of three boys. My brothers are five years and eleven years older than I am, and as the baby of the family, I don't recall a lot of tenderness going on in our brotherly relationships. One time I went into the bedroom of Warren, my oldest brother, who was also an amateur radio operator. Warren was on the radio, and I don't recall whether any of his friends were there or not. I just wanted to be in there with my big brother, but he said I had to get out of his room. I argued with him and he said, "I'm going to give you to a count of three to get out of here, and if you don't, you're in big trouble." He reached behind his door for his BB gun as he talked. As I quickly exited his room, I felt a burning sensation as a BB bounced off my backside. He lovingly said, "There you go, fat-butt," his loving, tender nickname for his baby brother. This is an illustration of the general lack of tenderness that exists in most families. By the way, Warren is a lot more tender to me today.

In chapter 3 we talked about the importance of showing affection to your children. While all siblings fight, tease, and even mistreat one another from time to time, showing tenderness in your home will help them learn to be kind and tender with one another, even if sibling tenderness doesn't show up until later. Parents can plant the seeds of tenderness and affection and water them with kindness, and then trust God to produce the blooms in their children.

We consider tenderness to be a form of weakness.
Even though we generally find tenderness in another person to be very attractive, it remains a foreign and uncomfortable concept in our own life. We are naturally attracted to pictures of Mother Teresa as she reaches out to tenderly touch diseased and dying people. While we recognize her as a very warm, loving, tender person, our culture usually elevates a "survivor" mentality. This can be seen in the popularity of TV's *Survivor* and other reality shows where people build alliances and teams for the purpose of winning. Winning is the goal in our culture, not showing tenderness, not losing in order that others might win, not caring for other people. We teach our children (and apply to ourselves) statements like, "Don't cry," "Don't let them see your weakness," or "Keep a stiff upper lip."

Being tender in a relationship requires a level of vulnerability that most people aren't comfortable with—especially men. Generally, women in our culture express tenderness more openly than men have been able to do.

Men are more likely to think tenderness is for losers, not winners, and we want to win at all cost. We've all heard the statement, "You need to toughen up." The idea of being yielding, soft, and broken is very unattractive.

We fear the responsibility that comes with being tender.
Whenever we reach out and touch another person physically and emotionally at their point of need, we're connecting at a level that requires some responsibility.

When a dad finds his fifteen-year-old daughter having a bad day and he expresses tenderness in the form of a hug and an offer to help, he's got to be willing to stay and engage in his daughter's life for a while. A pat on the head or an instruction on how to fix her problem is much easier for many dads than stopping and connecting. Personally, stopping to connect has never been easy for me.

When my daughter, Andrea, was a teenager she was more emotionally expressive than her two brothers were, and she often shared what she was going through. But instead of expressing tenderness by listening to her, hugging her, and sitting down to let her get her problems off her chest, I would usually tell her what she needed to do. Like many fathers, I thought my role was fixing problems instead of just being available.

We are just plain selfish.

It is easy to get caught up in our own priorities and miss one another's needs. In chapter 1, I mentioned Henry David Thoreau, who talked about the many people who live lives of quiet desperation. I think that's true in many of our families. We focus on our own priorities and ignore those of others around us.

One elderly woman had suffered from chronic illness for years. Her income was low, and her needs were great. But she was unflappably cheerful. When asked what kept her so upbeat, she said, "I volunteer at the children's hospital once a week, and seeing those little smiling faces keeps me going. And it keeps me thankful for what I have." This woman had learned the secret of getting the focus off of her own problems: Do something to help someone else and you'll forget yourself for at least a while.

We confuse physical intimacy (sex) with tenderness.

Tenderness during sex doesn't make you a tender person. It makes you a tender lover, but not necessarily a tender partner. What goes on outside the bedroom is what is most important. Tenderness must occur in the kitchen, in the laundry room, the family room, and out in the yard.

Tenderness is the genuine caring and empathy for your spouse that manifests itself all the time, not just during sex. It doesn't show itself in an attempt to progress to a sexual encounter, because that is fake and manipulative. True tenderness stands alone as a transparent display of care and love.

We look for substitutes for tenderness.
When I've had a difficult day or I'm feeling drained emotionally, my first thought is to pick up the phone and call Donna for a little TLC—tender loving care. She makes me feel cared for.

When we don't feel cared for, we look for substitutes for tenderness, many of which are self-destructive: alcohol, drugs, promiscuous sex, pornography, busyness, or shopping, among others. These substitutes never satisfy, because what we're really looking for is human connection and a sense of significance. We can find those in our relationships—not just marital relationships, but also those with friends, relatives, neighbors, and coworkers—and most important, in our relationship with God. Appropriately expressed, tenderness is a universal demonstration of love; people are attracted to tender people.

WHAT IF MY SPOUSE ISN'T TENDER?

The fact is that some people have tough hides. To them, the thought of being tender is foreign and frightening. But even Mr. or Ms. Armadillo-hide needs tenderness. What's a person to do?

If you have a tough cut of meat and want to make it edible, you can use tenderizing spices or a marinade or you can poke it with a fork or pound it with a meat hammer to tenderize it. But if you have a tough person, there's nothing you can do to tenderize him. Nagging, demanding, yelling, and pouting don't work and will probably drive him further into his hard shell. In my years of working with people, I've only discovered two things that can break through a tough hide: a personal relationship with Jesus Christ and challenging life experiences.

God as a tenderizer

When we put our faith in Christ, he gets to make us into new creatures. David asked God to "Create in me a clean heart" (Psalm 51:10). That clean, new heart that God gives us is tender or about to become tender.

Chuck Colson was the hatchet man for Richard Nixon in the White House Watergate scandal. As I understand it, he was pretty brutal in his relationships. His motto was "Win at all costs." But after facing the Watergate crisis and giving his life to Christ, this man's life was radically changed. He's still, I'm sure, a pretty tough businessman who knows how to get things done, but he has a tender heart and compassion for those in need. His organization, Prison Fellowship Ministry, through their Angel Tree program at Christmastime, delivers thousands of Christmas presents to the children of inmates from their parents in prison. Colson once had a tough hide, but God tenderized him through his conversion to Christ and his life experiences.

Life as a tenderizer

As much as we hate difficulty and tragedy and try to avoid them, God can use them to tenderize our heart and make us more like Jesus. My heart was broken when my dad died ten years ago, and it was the first time in my life that I started to really experience and express my feelings, even through tears.

I know of a wealthy woman who assumed her wealth would always be available—until she lost it all. As her material comforts slipped away one by one, she gained a new insight into what it must be like day in and day out for poor people who struggle to make ends meet and provide the bare necessities for their families. She became tenderized to the plight of others in a new way.

During hard times—the loss of a child, a job, a dream, or a relationship—we must choose to be either tender or tough, to let life harden or soften us toward God and others.

Can't I DO something?

Yes, you can. As I said, nagging and demanding won't do a bit of good to "tenderize" your spouse. What you can do is pray. Two books I've recommended over the years are Stormie Omartian's *The Power of a Praying Wife* and *The Power of a Praying Husband*, because prayer can break through a tough hide. I've seen it happen.

You can also show your spouse tenderness, even if it's uncomfortable for both of you. A tender touch, a kind word, a loving look when applied in the formula for tenderness can, over time, soften even a toughie.

You can speak from your heart to your spouse's heart to show him your need. If your spouse doesn't know how to give or receive tenderness, you might try a word picture to demonstrate how you feel when you receive tenderness. Perhaps many days you feel like it's July in the Mojave Desert and you're thirsty, tired, and wondering if you're going to survive the heat. Suddenly, your spouse smiles and takes your hand (and maybe even puts a glass of water into it) and you're amazingly refreshed, your hope renewed. Create your own word picture that would be meaningful to you and your spouse.

Finally, you can speak from your head to your spouse's head, telling him how to meet your needs.

One of my recurring themes in solving the problem of affection starvation is the need to be specific in letting our spouse know how to show affection and tenderness to us. For example, "You know, I want you to know how much it meant to me last night when you came through the kitchen and took just a second to touch my face and tell me you loved me. I really appreciated that." Don't let acts of tenderness go by without reinforcing the action and sharing with your spouse your need and appreciation for them.

If you are starved for affection, get to work on increasing the tenderness in your marriage. Express it to your spouse with appropriate physical touching, emotional touching, wise timing, and consistency. Whether or not you receive it in return, you will warm up your marriage by showing your spouse how it's done. And you will put in place one of the important building blocks upon which love, intimacy, trust, and affection can be built. It's always worth it to take time for tenderness.

THE TENDER FAMILY

The benefits of tenderness extend beyond marriage. Tenderness sends incredibly positive signals and teaches strong life lessons to our children. When they see Mom and Dad caring for each other with tenderness, boys learn how a woman is to be treated and daughters learn what to look for in a man.

When our children were younger and I'd give my wife a big hug in the kitchen, the kids would roll their eyes and say "Yuck!" They'd get embarrassed and tell us to go to our room. But they were really saying, "Thank you. We like this . . . we feel secure when you do that. Thank you for loving each other; it's providing security for us."

You can refer back to chapter 3 to review how affection in the family can be made stronger. Not only can you improve your marriage with regularly applied doses of tenderness, you can also increase the likelihood that your children's marriages will be tender and affectionate because they observed it at home.

Chapter 11

STARVED
FOR PASSION

Lust, greed, and manipulation—the entertainment media often portray sex as a combination of these. Unfortunately, this view has seeped into the Christian community as well. I've been a counselor working with people long enough to know that this whole issue of sexuality between a man and woman in marriage can be a huge problem, a problem you may have experienced in your marriage.

So to be practical, allow me to be explicit and straightforward but also bring us back to God's view of how sex is to work in a loving relationship between a man and a woman in marriage.

Sex is a taboo topic in far too many circles. Pastors seldom speak of it from the pulpit and counselors often shy away from addressing these issues. For many couples, it is a topic never discussed. We can talk about our children, our work, and a hundred other things, but to talk about the sexual part of us—a part that God created—is a topic we avoid. Yet the Bible speaks to it very clearly and directly. The best source of information on sexuality is the One who created it in the first place.

I once saw a woman interviewed on TV just before Valentine's Day who said, "Three times as many women would rather have a gift for Valentine's Day than to have sex with their spouse." My guess is that probably closer to eight or ten times as many women feel that way. According to Tim and Bev LaHaye in their book *The Act of Marriage after 40*, the three stages of a couple's love life are:

Couples in their twenties have sex tri-weekly.
Couples in their thirties try weekly.
Couples in their forties, fifties, and sixties try weakly![7]

As funny as this statement is, sexual intimacy is an important ingredient for a successful marriage, and it is encouraged by God.

God does desire Christian married couples to enjoy a healthy sexual relationship. It is one of the three important aspects of closeness and intimacy in marriage: spiritual, emotional, and physical (or sexual) intimacy. We talk about spiritual intimacy and emotional intimacy elsewhere in this book, but I need to again emphasize that these critical areas are strongly connected with physical intimacy and have a major influence on a couple's sexual relationship.

Most couples develop intimacy in reverse order from God's plan, starting at the physical level. We are attracted to another person and he or she meets some of our needs. We usually start at the physical level, perhaps progress to the emotional level, and then possibly the spiritual level. We decide to get married before we realize we are marrying the whole package.

I'm convinced that God designed us to do this in the reverse order, starting at the spiritual level and asking, "Are we compatible at the spiritual level? Does this person share the same faith I have? The same values? If so, can I connect with him or her at the soul level? Do we have emotional compatibility? The same interests? Do we share an intellectual interest in wanting to grow and develop?" We'll talk more about spiritual intimacy in chapter 14.

God designed physical intimacy to begin after marriage. Today many people become physically intimate before they have any intimacy at the emotional and spiritual level. Sixty-two percent of twenty-somethings say they believe it's important for a couple to live together before they get married so they really get to know each other. Not only is that the opposite of what God designed, but research shows it doesn't work. When you are physically intimate before you get married, the probability of divorce increases.

For those who are already married and were physically involved before marriage, you may not have connected emotionally or spiritually yet with your spouse. But it's not too late.

WHAT'S THE BIG DEAL?

Why is sexual intimacy so important in marriage? Sexual intimacy is important in marriage for many reasons. In this next section, we'll see how sexual intimacy provides protection against adultery, how it creates mutual satisfaction for both partners, and often leads to the creation of new life.

Protection against adultery

Human beings have sexual urges. Women, you know that being married to a typical man means dealing with strong sexual energy. I would hope that you, too, have strong sexual needs. Your husband needs sexual release and connection with you in marriage, and God designed it this way to keep us from fulfilling that need outside the marriage bond. In 1 Corinthians 7:1-2 (NIV) Paul says, "It is good for a man not to marry. But since there is so much immorality, each man should have his own wife, and each woman her own husband." Humans have such a powerful need for sexual relationship that if we don't have that in our marriage, the temptation—even in the believing community—to go outside the marriage to fulfill that need is very powerful. God wants us to fulfill our sexual needs within our marriage relationship. Unfortunately, many people go outside the marriage because their needs are not being met in the marriage.

If you are not meeting the needs of your spouse, if you are not sexually active and involved in the process of intimacy, you are exposing yourself, your marriage, and your spouse to great danger. Don't kid yourself. If you are saying, "Hey, sex isn't important to me," "I don't like sex," or "She wants it more often than I do," you both need to sit down and figure out how to become passionate lovers together. If you don't, you are setting yourselves up for exposure to danger in your marriage. A main reason God created sex within marriage was to protect us from extramarital affairs or adultery outside marriage.

The spice of married life

God designed sex to be pleasurable and satisfying to both partners in the marital context. If you don't enjoy sex in your marriage, get help. God did not make us to live a lifetime of misery brought on by the sexual side of our marriage.

A book of the Bible that you seldom hear preached from is the Song of Solomon, which is a picture of the love of a man for a woman, and a woman for a man. The book's picturesque wording describes what happens between this man and woman in marriage in chapter 4, verses 10-16 (NIV):

How delightful is your love, my sister, my bride! How much more pleasing is your love than wine, and the fragrance of your perfume than any spice! Your lips drop sweetness as the honeycomb, my bride; milk and honey are under your tongue. The fragrance of your garments is like that of Lebanon. You are a garden locked up, my sister, my bride; you are a spring enclosed, a sealed fountain. Your plants are an orchard of pomegranates with choice fruits, with henna and nard, nard and saffron, calamus and cinnamon, with every kind of incense tree, with myrrh and aloes and all the finest spices. You are a garden fountain, a well of flowing water streaming down from Lebanon.

[Now the bride speaks:] Awake, north wind, and come, south wind! Blow on my garden, that its fragrance may spread abroad. Let my lover come into his garden and taste its choicest fruits.

What a picture! This man describes his attraction to this woman, his lover, his friend, and she expresses her desire for him. If you read this book in the Bible, you see that God describes a beautiful, intimate experience between a man and a woman in marriage and he designed sexual intimacy in marriage to include mutual satisfaction. During the act of sexual intercourse and orgasm, there is a release of powerful hormones in the brain. They are even called a kind of love potion or love hormones, because after the act of intercourse a feeling of closeness or intimacy occurs physiologically for both a man and a woman. God designed this closeness to reinforce their bond.

One of the problems in a marriage where a couple doesn't enjoy each another sexually is that they don't experience this completeness. If one of the spouses then experiences an emotional connection with someone else outside of marriage, the bonding God intended for spouses begins to occur with the wrong person. One of the reasons God is so opposed to extramarital or premarital sex or promiscuity is that he knows that sex affects our emotions. Those of you who married as virgins don't have that emotional connection with individuals in your past. But for those who were sexually active before marriage, a battle with memories and powerful emotions often goes on in the back of your mind. Sexual memories between a husband and wife provide a sense of closeness, but memories of the past can haunt you years into your marriage. Ask God to free you from memories of people other than your spouse so that you can enjoy the closeness and satisfaction that comes from a good sexual relationship in your marriage.

Mom, Dad . . . and kids

A basic, practical aspect of sexual intimacy is reproduction. In Genesis 1:28 (NIV) God blessed and instructed Adam and Eve, saying, "Be fruitful and increase in number; fill the earth and subdue it." God designed sex in marriage to be a part of the creation of children. One of the reasons God objects to sexual immorality is that producing children is not any part of it, placing it outside of God's plan. That doesn't mean every time we have sex in marriage our goal is to have children. If that were true, statistically we could potentially have more than three thousand children over our lifetime! Nor does it mean that every couple will have children. But God's design for a man and woman in marriage is that the outcome certainly could be procreation. That's one reason God hates extramarital affairs where there is no intention to have children. Sex outside of marriage is not a part of a giving, caring, loving, committed relationship. It is selfish, based on what each person wants at the time.

GOD'S PLAN FOR SEX

Since God intends for married couples to have a good sexual relationship in order to protect the marriage, to provide pleasure and satisfaction to the couple, and to produce children, he makes a way for that to happen. What does God expect from lovers in marriage? How do they reach this level of satisfying sex? In order to have a satisfying sexual relationship in marriage, God calls spouses to *exclusivity*, *frequency*, and *sensitivity*.

Just you and me

First, God wants exclusivity—no one but your spouse should share in any form of intimacy with you. In Hebrews 13:4, we read that we are to keep the marriage bed pure. God's design is for us to be with one person, sexually, emotionally, and spiritually in marriage for a lifetime. One reason I object so strongly to pornography is that it stimulates the mind and thoughts, causing sexual and emotional dissatisfaction because most people cannot live up to the photographs that have been retouched, enhanced, and manipulated to give us an image of perfection. Indulging in pornography is not exclusivity.

At one time and probably today as well, couples engaged in spouse swapping—sharing spouses in sexual relations. God hates that because his Word says we are to keep the marriage bed pure. Whenever we go outside our marriage for sexual relationships, it's sin. In 1 Corinthians 6:18-20 (NIV), the apostle Paul says, "Flee from sexual immorality. All other sins a man commits are outside his body, but he who sins sexually sins against his own body. Do you not know that your body is a temple of the Holy Spirit, who is in you, whom you have received from God? You are not your own; you were bought at a price. Therefore honor God with your body."

God says when we have sex outside of our marriage it's a sin in a class all by itself. It's different from stealing, lying, or being dishonest. When you engage in sexual immorality, you bring the sin into your body. You become one flesh with the other person, not only emotionally but also physically. And in the process you violate God's property. Since we belong to God, we are his property and we are the temple of the Holy Spirit who lives in us. Would we go to our church on Sunday dirty, and be crude, rude, and nasty? I hope not. And yet we do that with the temple, our own body God has given us, the exclusive property of the Holy Spirit. God clearly tells us to be exclusive in our marriage relationship.

How often?
What does God say about frequency of sex in marriage? We know from research and from personal experience that men and women are generally different. Some women would be happy with sexual relations once a year. There are guys who would prefer sex once every hour. God wired men and women very differently, and we can balance each other out.

But he does talk about frequency. In 1 Corinthians 7:3-5 (NIV), Paul says, "The husband should fulfill his marital duty to his wife, and likewise the wife to her husband. The wife's body does not belong to her alone but also to her husband. In the same way, the husband's body does not belong to him alone but also to his wife. Do not deprive each other except by mutual consent and for a time, so that you may devote yourselves to prayer. Then come together again so that Satan will not tempt you because of your lack of self control."

That passage says that as a married couple we are to have sex, then we are to fast and pray, and then we are to have sex again. I don't know how else to put it, but God is saying that frequency counts. Being involved with each other sexually in marriage counts because we live in a world of tremendous temptation that would pull us away from that sexual and emotional bond with our spouse.

In the LaHayes' book *The Act of Marriage after 40* a husband, Billy Bob, said,

> We are in our mid-fifties and our sex life is "old hat." I was doing the math the other day, some mental calculations, and figuring that we made love twice a week and that's around a hundred times a year. Now multiply that by thirty and add a few hundred times for those first exciting years of marriage, and I come away with a figure of 3,300 times that Agnes and I made love. If you do something 3,300 times over a course of a lifetime, even something as physical, intense, and exciting as sexual intercourse, there is a tendency to go through the motions. Lovemaking is always the same; at least it's been that way since our first child was born twenty-five years ago.

Billy Bob speaks for a lot of men: Years of living together, going to work, raising kids, and taking care of life's responsibilities and sex can become routine. Of course, only a guy would sit down and run the math. I can imagine one of you saying, "Wait a minute, I'm only up to 2,700; I'm not up with old Billy Bob."

Billy Bob's wife, Agnes, said,

> You mean my husband has made love with me only 3,300 times? He has to be joking. If we had sexual relations every time he wanted to, that number would be 33,000. Frankly, I'm tired of sex! Been there and done

that. A half a dozen times a year would be fine for me. I could even handle once a month if he ever got off his duff and wined and dined me for a change.[8]

I hear again and again that all the husband wants is sex. His wife asks, "Why doesn't he care for me? When we are not in bed he is not showing appreciation for me, he is not loving me, he is not showing affection to me." Let me just say this: Guys, if you are not emotionally "wining and dining" your spouse, getting to know her, understanding how she sees life, you are missing the fact that your sexual relationship in marriage is not all it can be. You are missing out on "wooing" your wife in the process of lovemaking. God intends for us to woo our wife. It's part of leadership, drawing our spouse into that kind of intimacy and closeness that God meant to occur between a man and woman in marriage. We'll talk more in the next chapter about an exercise that will draw you closer together physically and nonsexually as well.

I came across one writer to "Dear Abby" who admitted that after thirty years of marriage, she could live without sex altogether. Believing that most women "go through the motions [of sex]," the writer challenged the columnist to poll readers and confirm her suspicions. The response was overwhelming and a significant percentage agreed with the original letter writer. One male respondent, who found the results both astounding and depressing, considered such a sexual charade as a form of emasculation.

I think many men can relate, because after years and years of feeling coldness and rejection from their wives in the sexual area of their relationship, they start to lose their desire and interest—they give up. On the other hand, I've had many women say to me, "But Randy, you don't understand! My husband is gross; he doesn't take care of himself, he doesn't know how to express love!"

We can probably agree that men and women see the issue very differently, but God designed a balance between men and women in marriage, a balance that gives satisfaction to both partners. If you are not experiencing sexual excitement, mutual satisfaction, closeness, and frequency appropriate in marriage, then make a commitment to get to know your spouse. Spend time together, talking about the things that mean the most to him or her. Tim and Bev LaHaye surveyed couples between ages forty and seventy and found that the average couple had sexual intercourse three times a month, more often for those closer to forty, and even more frequently for much younger couples. But the average frequency, depending on age, is about twice a week. This figure can be used as a benchmark, but it is not a hard-and-fast rule. Each couple must decide what is right for their marriage.

The importance of feelings

Besides exclusivity and frequency, God also expects sensitivity toward your spouse's feelings. I get questions about masturbation, oral sex, and many other topics—about what is appropriate or not appropriate in a marriage relationship. In some cases God's Word is clear, and in others it is not. But there's a principle in God's Word that says we are never to do anything that's an offense to a person we love (Philippians 1:9-10). We are to be sensitive to her needs and viewpoints, never forcing our spouse to do anything in marriage, sexually or otherwise, that would be contrary to how she feels or how she interprets Scripture. The Bible says in Ephesians 5:21 that we are to mutually submit to one another. The idea of sexual intimacy in marriage is not only what we get but what we give—where there's a willingness to not only share ourselves but to please our spouse emotionally and physically. When we do that instead of thinking just of our own interests, we are pleasing God. He designed the marital sexual relationship to work best when each spouse is more interested in giving than receiving. Being sensitive to the needs of our spouse is crucial.

Another principle involves the biblical instruction to refrain from lust. One of the problems with an activity like masturbation is that it typically involves lust and selfishness. There's no Bible verse that says, "Thou shalt not masturbate." But the Bible does say, in a Randy Carlson paraphrase of Matthew 5:28, "Thou shalt not lust, thou shalt not look on a woman to lust after her because if you've done that, that's already sin." The average person who masturbates experiences lust, and that's the sin. It's thinking of our own interests and not those of our spouse.

MOVING FORWARD

So how do we achieve exclusivity, frequency, and sensitivity? God desires personal purity, and he also wants sex to be fun and spontaneous. If married couples strive for both of these things, it will be easier for them to be exclusive, sensitive to the other, and to have sex frequently.

When Billy Bob talked about his years of marriage and raising kids, it was a reminder that routine can wear you down. Any of us who have raised kids while working to provide for the family, know that the sexual relationship in marriage can seem like nothing more than just a routine. It becomes fulfillment of a hormonal reaction, a physical release and response instead of something God designed for us as a creative, fun, and spontaneous part of our marriage.

I've heard some great ideas from creative people on my radio show who do something extra for their spouse. One guy leaves a note for his wife every morning and another leaves the garage door open for his wife every night. One guy calls his wife two or three times every day, just to tell her he's thinking about her. Donna rubs my back when I come home from work because the physical touch makes us feel closer. If the lovemaking in your marriage is the same as the way you did it five or ten years ago and you are not doing things differently, you are missing out on what God designed to be creative and fun.

Research shows that young married couples have intercourse much more often than older people do. But the research is also clear that when couples have been married thirty or forty years, when they do have sexual relations, it's much more satisfying because they have learned how to give and receive. Let's face it—when we were twenty or twenty-five years old, we still were hormone happy and had not yet learned how to give and receive in marriage. But an older couple, who have been married many years and have achieved intimacy with each other, may have sex just a few times each year but their closeness and creativity in knowing how to please each other is a beautiful thing.

OBSTACLES TO SEXUAL INTIMACY IN MARRIAGE

Tim and Bev LaHaye list problems that can negatively impact the sexual relationship: fatigue; depression; stress; anger; and negative thoughts about yourself, your marriage, or your life, among other issues.

Another problem is unattractiveness. I hear frequently, "When I married him he was neat and clean; now he comes home greasy and dirty; he smells and doesn't take care of himself (or herself)." God intended us not only to be attracted to our spouse, but to be attractive for our spouse. Of course, our body changes over the years and attraction changes as well, but God still meant for us to do everything we possibly can to be attractive for and attracted to our spouse.

Criticism is also a problem. Often when a couple is trying to be close, one criticizes the other: "You're not doing this" or "You should have done that" or "You are a bad parent" or "Why do you do this all the time?" Often the guy will criticize one moment and think sex can fix it the next. Yet once there is criticism in a relationship, the average woman's interest needle plummets way below zero.

A number of health conditions can impact sexual relationships, but the vast majority of couples can still achieve emotional and physical intimacy.

Medications can also affect the sexual relationship. If you take one or more medications, talk to the pharmacist to find out if any of them create a problem for you in responding sexually to your spouse. Medication for high blood pressure and other types of conditions can produce sexual side effects, including reduced desire. Certain illnesses, such as diabetes, can create serious problems in the sexual area of marriage. Back problems, pain, discomfort, and erectile dysfunction cause other problems. If you have problems with sexual performance in your marriage, see a doctor to make sure there is not a medical concern that can be helped.

But what about the frequent problem mentioned—particularly among women—a recurring "lack of interest" even where no health problems exist? I often hear comments like, "I'm just not interested; sex could just go away and it would be fine with me!" "I want to be emotionally close and spiritually close, and I would like to have sexual interest, but I don't!" Emotional problems also affect the sexual relationship in marriage. Seeing a counselor can help get to the root of these difficulties.

One report shows that nearly 75 percent of women feel embarrassed about their body and don't see themselves as their husband sees them. But if you've got a loving, caring husband who loves you—he loves you! One man told his wife, "Instead of letting the mirror be your mirror, let me be your mirror; let me reflect who you really are." If you have a fear of rejection or you grew up in a home where there was abuse, neglect, or lack of affection you may struggle with emotional problems that prevent you from seeing sex as God designed it for marriage. Find a friend or counselor who understands what you are going through, what you are struggling with, and knows how to help you deal with it.

DANGER—LOOK OUT!

Because we love our spouse, because we love God and our marriage, we should be willing to deal with our spiritual problems, our physical problems (when possible), and our emotional problems in order to be what God wants us to be in marriage—sexually active with our spouse. If you find that there are physical roadblocks to the kind of sexual intimacy you would like, and they cannot be cured, you need to accept that and move on with your life, continuing to love and care for your spouse. And if you get to a point where there are emotional roadblocks, say, *Dear Lord, I accept where I am and I will remain faithful.* God never gave us an "out" in this area. He doesn't say, "Hey, if you're married to a person who has emotional problems and doesn't want to be involved sexually as much as you would like, or it's not fulfilling for your needs, then you can get out of this marriage and go find someone who is going to meet your needs." As a Christian, if you're married and you are not finding satisfaction in the sexual area, get help! It's of utmost importance.

We violate our marriage when we are more intimate on any level—spiritually, emotionally, or physically—with another person than we are with our spouse. Ask yourself this question, and answer honestly: Is there anyone in your life who knows you better than your spouse knows you? If there is, that's a serious potential problem. And if you're more intimate with another human being than you are with your spouse in any area of your life, you're playing with fire and asking to get burned.

It would be far better to be unfulfilled in one of these areas and resist the temptation to be intimate with another person than to meet that need outside of marriage, becoming vulnerable to failure in our lifetime commitment. When you get outside your marriage, you're setting yourself up for disaster.

Rich told me that he and his wife had let work take over their lives and they forgot how to talk to each other. He said, "She found an old friend and had been talking more to him than me and let it get carried away—not physically but verbally. We kind of lost our way for a long time. Now we're struggling to find each other again. I'm trying to believe it's all done and she's bringing everything back to me, but it's hard to believe that still. It was a wake-up call to both of us."

We are most vulnerable at our weakest point. If you are not having sexual intimacy in your marriage, your marriage is vulnerable at the sexual level. If you don't have soul intimacy where you share the same intellectual interests and emotional connection, you are vulnerable in that area. Couples don't need to have all the same interests in order to connect effectively, but it's wise to be aware of your differences and realize that unless your marriage is strong, someone who clicks with

you in an area of dissimilarity in your marriage could be dangerous for you. When you're at work or you're at church and someone starts to meet your emotional needs, it's easy to get sucked
right into it.

Every one of us is potentially vulnerable to that kind of situation, no matter how spiritual we are. Satan loves to attack us
where we're weakest, and you can be sure he will. If you're having great spiritual intimacy in your marriage, that's probably
not where you're going to be attacked. But if you have lousy
emotional intimacy or soul intimacy in your marriage, Satan is
going to hit you there. What is the weakest link in your marriage? Is it spiritual intimacy, soul intimacy, or body intimacy?
Once you know what it is, be on your guard, and get to work to
strengthen that area. Identifying areas of weakness is the first
step in strengthening and overcoming them.

The more you know someone, the deeper the intimacy
should become. You should be more intimate today than you
were a year ago. If you've been married more than a few years, is
your intimacy getting deeper and richer in each of these areas,
or are you finding that it's stagnant—not moving or growing?
Stagnation can be a killer in marriage.

Again, if you are struggling in the area of sexual fulfillment
in your marriage, first talk with your spouse and then get some
help so that you can enjoy the rich relationship God designed
for both of you.

Chapter 12

STARVED FOR NONSEXUAL AFFECTION

Do you long for a back rub from your spouse that doesn't lead to sex? Or a nonsexual snuggling session on the couch as you watch a movie together? Does it seem like the only time the two of you touch each other is in preparation for sex? You might have an active sexual relationship with your spouse, but you could be starved for nonsexual affection.

If so, you're going to need to talk about it openly with your spouse. Let him know that while you, too, want to enjoy great sex together, you also need more nonsexual affection than you're getting now. Explain that you know of a plan that can increase the quality of both your sexual relationship and your nonsexual affection, so that both of you wind up getting what you need and desire.

This can be a difficult subject to discuss. Pick a calm, quiet time and place to talk with your spouse about the fact that both sexual and nonsexual affection is really important to you. I believe your spouse will listen.

We've seen that often sex is the way a spouse, usually the man, communicates in his marriage. To him, sex is affection, conversation, and closeness all rolled up into one. He may not even realize that you're lacking anything and need more from him, and expressing your needs will let him know. What you are about to tell him can provide him with the sexual fulfillment he desires while meeting your needs as well.

If you are starved for nonsexual affection, but you do not have the support of your spouse in trying to make your marriage more affectionate, I'd suggest showing him or her the kind of nonsexual affection you would like to receive. By making this movement in his direction, you might open the door to talking at a later time about trying a time of fasting from sexual relations.

DEFEATING MEDIOCRITY

No one wants anything ordinary or commonplace. Ever heard anyone rave about a dinner that's only so-so? Or brag about driving a car that's second-rate? In our world, there's no room for anything unimpressive, passable, or average. And that's especially true when it comes to sex. That's exactly what thousands of couples experience, day after day, year after year. I hear from them all the time on my radio program: men frustrated because they find their wives boring in bed; women distraught because it seems like every physical touch or encounter leads to sex.

So what's the solution? How can both partners receive what they need: nonsexual affection *and* sexual fulfillment? Does the answer lie in improved technique, a new acrobatic position, or some magic pill? Nope . . . I believe the key to transforming sex from ordinary to extraordinary rests in good old-fashioned discipline and denial. It's being sure that *both* of you get what you need.

A FAILURE TO COMMUNICATE

As I said, solving this problem requires honest and clear communication. The biggest problem of an "intercourse focused" relationship is that it usually results in one, or both, partners suffering from a failure to communicate affectionately. The sense of closeness so necessary in a marriage—a tender touch, a helping hand, a word of respect and appreciation—may be desperately lacking. When nonsexual acts of affection constantly lead to intercourse, one of the following three scenarios generally plays out:

1. The couple responds with great sexual passion and enjoyment—but that's all there is. Their intimacy is hollow, superficial, and solely physical. There's no substance beyond the sex.
2. Sexual intercourse climaxes with only one of the partners feeling satisfied intimately. The other is left holding a bag devoid of respect and affection. That person may have made love, but he or she doesn't *feel* loved.
3. One of the partners will put up an emotional guard and refuse sex, leaving both people unhappy. Rejection runs through the veins of the sexually interested partner, while the other spouse just resents being used.

As you talk about a strategy for improving your sexual relationship, let your spouse know that receiving nonsexual affection makes you feel a lot more like having great sex. In other words, there's something in this exercise for him!

Tell your spouse about some of these practical ways he can communicate affection to you effectively or do some of them for him:

🎴 Take a "vision walk," when you walk hand in hand sharing your dreams for the future.

- ❀ Talk to each other about the challenges and triumphs of your week, and then pray about them together.
- ❀ Draw a warm bath complete with candles and soft music . . . and then leave your spouse alone to enjoy it.
- ❀ Find a book of shared interest—anything from a novel to a devotional or the Bible—and read it out loud to each other.
- ❀ Snuggle—holding and even caressing your spouse's body without trying to provoke a sexual response. If either of you should become aroused in the process, keep it to yourself.
- ❀ Do something your spouse has wanted done for a long time—perhaps a chore around the house. It's best if this is something that requires some sacrifice, which will make it even more meaningful.

I mentioned old-fashioned discipline and denial at the beginning of this chapter. But how can that improve your sex life and your nonsexual affection? I know it will because I've seen it happen. What I'm talking about is a *sexual fast*, which means to refrain from having sex by mutual consent for an agreed upon period, such as one week, in order to focus on improving both the sexual and nonsexual affection in your marriage.

Here are five things I strongly believe a sexual fast can do for your marriage:

1. It can eliminate the fear of a sexual "sneak attack."
2. It can remove the barrier of expectations for sexual performance.
3. It can create self-discipline for the more sexually interested spouse.

4. It can demonstrate to your partner that you respect his needs.

5. It *will* produce an environment for nonsexual exploration of affection, replacing old patterns of relating to one another with new ones.

Thanks a lot, Carlson! your spouse may think. *You've just given my frigid spouse the ammunition she's been looking for. She didn't want sex in the first place . . . or any place, for that matter.*

But I've seen incredible results over the years with couples who have tried a sexual fast and are now enjoying exciting, consistent, impassioned, strip-the-paint-off-the-wall sex . . . that is wonderfully loving and fulfilling for both partners. In the process, they've also learned something about the mind of the sexually less-responsive spouse that has revolutionized their relationship.

But don't just take my word for it. Take a look at this encouraging account from a couple whose sex lives had been trapped in a prison of mediocrity, despite the fact that they had sex nearly *all* the time.

MAKING A CHANGE

For all of their nine years of marriage, Betsy couldn't even snuggle up next to Derek on the couch without setting him off. "Don't get me wrong," Betsy told me. "I enjoy sex. I wish we could just *be* together without it turning into something more."

Sadly, Derek was missing out on something really good. Betsy desired her husband and wanted a closer relationship with him. She was a reservoir of affection just waiting to be poured out, but Derek's sexually meteoric response to any kind of attention from his wife turned off the tap.

A date night ended in sex. Conversation about their day ended in sex. Sitting together at home and watching a football game resulted in sex during halftime. Even arguments ended with sex. All this made Betsy completely self-protective. She was always on guard because she had been trained that any overture she made to Derek, no matter how nonsexual, would lead directly to intercourse.

It was straight to sex jail. Do not pass Go. Do not collect $200.

Derek had also discovered that quantity did not mean quality. Sure, he got lots of sex—but very little fulfillment. Overall, Derek was a no-nonsense kind of guy who was notorious for driving through to the bottom line, so initiating sex came naturally to him. But he approached sex as a project, not a passion, and was insensitive to Betsy's need for nonsexual affection. As a result, she was totally uninvolved emotionally during lovemaking, leaving Derek feeling somehow empty and incomplete.

When I suggested they try a sexual fast, Betsy latched on to the idea right away. While desperate to do anything to help their fading relationship, Betsy also saw the immediate, short-term benefit of the fast—time off! Derek, on the other hand, wasn't terribly enthusiastic about the plan, but because he, too, saw the downward direction of the marriage, he didn't see any harm in humoring me by going along.

Together, they agreed to a seven-day fast without intercourse. That's no sex for 168 hours, or 10,080 minutes. Derek did the math.

When I spelled out the specific strategy for their fast, I made sure there would be a proper balance between his needs and her needs. Each day they would spend a predetermined amount of time together experimenting with various expressions of affection, without expectation of intercourse. Once I got them over the hurdle of accepting the fast, Betsy and Derek were off and running. Here was the plan:

Day One: Take a walk together with each person sharing one dream and one fear for the future—without evaluation, criticism, or correction.

Day Two: Go out of the way to anticipate a specific need of the other and meet it before it's even mentioned, doing so without receiving a pat on the back (or anywhere else).

Day Three: Give each other a back rub, foot massage, or some other expression of enjoyable physical touch, and stay disciplined if the activity leads to sexual arousal.

Day Four: Discuss five things they would like to accomplish or experience as a couple before they die. After the discussion, write out a brief plan that could make each of those dreams a reality.

Day Five: Take a long bath or shower together—without sex.

Day Six: Go out to dinner and discuss what the past five days has meant to each and to their marriage.

Day Seven: Do something to surprise each other. Buy a special gift, write a poem or love note, or make an unexpected call to the other person.

Day Eight: Have Betsy (because she's the least sexually interested of the couple) plan a romantic experience and take the lead in initiating sex . . . and enjoy!

I knew Betsy and Derek would only make it through those seven days if they stretched themselves. Betsy wasn't a physically expressive woman. In fact, she was quite reserved, so I figured standing totally naked—and unprotected—in front of her husband in the shower, or allowing him to freely massage her skin with oil and powder would be downright scary for her.

Because Derek was an emotionally closed man, I thought the sexual fast would certainly expand him outside his safety zone and force him to see Betsy and their relationship beyond his comfortable and familiar sexual boundaries. The seven-day plan was also designed to help Betsy and Derek take a few positive steps toward new ways of relating to each other and break them out of their patterned relationship, if only for one week.

In order for a sexual fast to be successful, it must not only be challenging for both partners, but it must also have elements of pleasure. Just the thought of having Betsy with him in the shower brought gratification to Derek, even though he knew sex would be off-limits. If anything, this enhanced his excitement. For Betsy, the anticipation of times of conversation during the week raised her interest in the experiment, even as it also forced her to cover some new territory in their relationship.

So how did Betsy and Derek fare on their fast? By the end of the week, they had not only survived, but thrived. They were learning how to love one another again in new and satisfying ways. It had begun with small steps, but they were now on the right path. I'd love to take the credit, but they did all the work.

Derek showed Betsy that he hadn't forgotten how to show nonsexual affection to her and he actually introduced new forms of pleasure to the marriage. Betsy knew there were times Derek's passion meter was going through the roof, but each time he exercised self-control, she said she immediately felt closer to him. More than that, Betsy was really impressed with Derek's new attitude toward affection as he made a concerted effort to show more interest in conversation, sharing, and playing together without sex being the end result. She now refers to her husband as "the new Derek."

Derek reaped the benefits of his turnaround. In the months

following the fast, he and Betsy made love a lot, almost as much as they did before, but the sex was better. Now that Betsy was being fulfilled affectionately in other ways, she was set free from her sexual jail. She also became more relaxed and expressive, and therefore started venturing out from her protective shell.

"When I started to show Betsy more attention outside the bedroom," Derek happily noted, "she started to show more passion in the bedroom. When we have sex now, it seems more exciting for us."

AN INTIMACY INCUBATOR

Betsy and Derek had discovered a wonderful truth. A sexual fast is a time when couples travel together into new levels of physical, emotional, and even spiritual familiarity, sharing, and closeness. The fast becomes an incubator for marital intimacy—an environment where the couple focuses on each other in new ways.

When all roads don't lead to sex, a whole new vocabulary of love often develops that's both healthy and enlightening for both partners. Suddenly, you have the freedom to say and hear statements of caring such as, "You look nice tonight" or "Come on over and sit next to me" or even "I love you" without having a cloud of sexual suspicion hanging over your head. A kiss is a kiss. A hug is a hug. A touch is a touch, nothing more.

Patty, a listener to my radio program, said she and her husband, Jim, were practicing natural family planning. This rhythm method of birth control requires them to abstain from sex for specific periods of time each month. Patty said the freedom from sexual expectation during those periods heightens their desire for each other and causes them to journey into realms of nonsexual expression they otherwise might never have discovered. Jim now understands the joy and satisfaction of expressing love to his wife without sex, and has found great pleasure in giving her long back rubs and cuddling up to her on the couch.

"Those times are very precious to me and have revitalized our marriage," said Patty. "Now, when it's time for sex, I'm usually not only ready, but looking forward to it. I've even become the initiator at times. I know Jim likes that."

When a couple gives sex too much importance, it can inhibit the development of emotional and conversational intimacy because it seems to be all about sex. Philip and Sherry wed right out of college, and in the nine years since had done nothing but struggle in their marriage. Sherry viewed their relationship as "intercourse focused." Like Betsy, it wasn't that Sherry didn't enjoy making love; she just found it hard to find the motivation.

"He expects me to be turned on in the bedroom when he's done nothing outside the bedroom to turn me on," she said.

Philip, on the other hand, saw nothing but his own sexual frustration. "If she's in the mood, then we'll have sex," he said bluntly. "If she's not, we don't." Philip felt that Sherry manipulated their relationship by controlling the frequency of sex.

When I proposed that they try a sexual fast, Philip reacted harshly. "If Sherry had her way, our entire marriage would be a sexual fast. She thinks all I want from her is sex anyway, which isn't true. In fact, I get very little from her as it is, and now it sounds like you're giving her an excuse to build some sort of a sexual hideout from me." He gave me the look of a man ready to do harm.

I immediately tried to reassure him, saying that a sexual fast is not intended to be a hideaway. I pressed the fact that a sexually healthy marriage has a lot more going for it than just great sex and that, in reality, quality sex is the result of healthy marriage—not the other way around. I'm sure Sherry was thinking, *Thank you, God! I finally have someone who agrees that men put too much focus on sex.*

But that wasn't my point, either. Sex *is* a big deal in marriage. A good sex life *is* important to a strong relationship and represents a vital part of affection. But sex has its rightful place and cannot be the sole focus of a marriage. Sadly, sex had become nothing more than a contest to Sherry and Philip, a battle of wills that neither could win.

SACKCLOTH AND ASHES?

If you and your spouse are willing to give this unorthodox sexual fast idea a go, let me lay out a few ground rules, the first of which is to go into it with the *right attitude*. In the Bible, the patriarchs would often enter a period of fasting rather dramatically: tearing their clothes, pulling out their hair, and donning a wardrobe of sackcloth and ashes.

Now, maybe the sight of your spouse in sackcloth and ashes could indeed kill your libido for a week or so. But instead of going to such extremes, embark on your sexual fast the way Christ encouraged people to fast for their spiritual development: "When you fast, do not look somber as the hypocrites do, for they disfigure their faces to show men they are fasting. . . . But when you fast, put oil on your head and wash your face, so that it will not be obvious to men that you are fasting, but only to your Father, who is unseen; and your Father, who sees what is done in secret, will reward you" (Matthew 6:16-18 NIV).

The principle is this: Don't enter into your period of sexual fasting as if it were a time of mourning, sorrow, and negativity. Instead, look at all the positive results it will have. Just as abstaining from food to devote yourself to a specific season of prayer will challenge you spiritually and deepen your walk with God, your sexual fast will foster discipline, create self-awareness, and enhance and strengthen your relationship with your spouse. It won't be easy, and it will stretch you, but the payoff may be life-changing!

A KEY INGREDIENT FOR SUCCESS

The ninth chapter of Mark records the account of Christ healing a demon-possessed boy after his disciples had failed to deliver the child from Satan's power. When the disciples later asked Jesus why they couldn't drive out the evil spirit, the Lord responded, "This kind can come out by nothing but prayer and fasting" (Mark 9:29). The biblical model of spiritual fasting is always accompanied by prayer, which leads into my second ground rule for your sexual fast: *Don't forget to pray.*

The apostle Paul endorses this dynamic combination of abstinence and supplication in his letter to the Corinthian church. First, he establishes how you are to serve your spouse in your physical relationship. He wrote, "The husband should fulfill his marital duty to his wife, and likewise the wife to her husband. The wife's body does not belong to her alone but also to her husband. In the same way, the husband's body does not belong to him alone but also to his wife" (1 Corinthians 7:3-4, NIV).

Paul clearly saw marriage as a decision to give up exclusive rights to your body. You are not only to share your body with your spouse, but also allow him or her access, each of you striking the right balance between giving and taking.

Then Paul makes his case for a sexual fast and its justification. "Do not deprive each other except by mutual consent and for a time, so that you may devote yourselves to prayer. Then come together again so that Satan will not tempt you because of your lack of self-control" (1 Corinthians 7:5, NIV).

Paul knew that prayer has to be a living, vital part of a Christian's lifestyle, so he proposed that couples leave sex behind for a while so they can better focus on their communication with God via prayer.

Before I lay out the basic elements necessary for your sexual fast, let me emphasize this: Your fast will be markedly more effective, more spiritually relevant—more *empowered*—when you incorporate prayer into the mix. Intercede for each other and pray for yourself, that God would do his cleansing and restorative work in your marriage through the fast. Remember that one of the most intimate things you can ever do is to pray for and with your spouse.

ENTERING THE FAST LANE

Your sexual fast can be as creative as you and your spouse want it to be, but here are the elements it must include:

- **Agreement** by both partners on all aspects of the fast.
- A particular **time limit**. In 1 Corinthians 7, Paul didn't address exactly how long to abstain from sex, except to say that it be only for a set time. It could last for one or two days a week, a week each month—whatever you feel is best, as long as it's specific.
- A willingness to explore **other areas of affection**. The greatest thing about a sexual fast is what it *doesn't* mean—a break from intimate expressions of love. It's only the intercourse that's put on hold. The length of time isn't as important as the effort you put into em-

phasizing areas of intimacy other than intercourse that will bring both emotional and physical pleasure. Throw in some spontaneity and surprises. And, as difficult as it may be, make sure to include activities that will take you out of your comfort zone.

- **Sex remains off-limits** for the entire period of the fast, even if you're both ready and eager to succumb. If you have to, literally get away from each other until you've cooled off sexually. Stay committed to abstinence, and build that discipline!
- End the fast by coming **back together sexually**.

A couple of quick words of encouragement, first for the *less* sexually interested spouse. For your sexual fast to work, you must join your partner in building closeness in your marriage by agreeing to leave your past behind and enter into your sexual relationship with a new fervor. This will not take place overnight, nor will it automatically just happen after concluding your first sexual fast.

But if you're someone like Sherry, who has used your sexuality as a weapon for control against your spouse, you must lay down your shield and give up the fight. Also, don't assume that your sexually focused spouse doesn't have a need for nonsexual affection, too. You need to work with him to uncover those areas of intimacy and begin meeting them. It will be wonderfully liberating for both of you.

If you're the *more* sexually interested individual in the marriage, I believe you should be the one to take the lead in making your sexual fast a reality. Don't be surprised if your mate thinks you've lost your mind, or initially does not even take your suggestion seriously. That's okay because when you follow through and voluntarily offer to throttle your sex passions in order to learn how to give your spouse the kind of pleasure she needs, it will increase your credibility. When you complete the fast, it'll show an incredible amount of love and sacrifice to your affection-hungry partner and will make a positive difference in your relationship.

Often when I suggest a sexual fast to couples, the husband hates the idea, and the wife loves it. This was also true of Philip and Sherry at first. But they both misread the reason for the exercise. She thought it meant sex wasn't important, and he thought I was saying that no sex was okay in marriage. Both were wrong.

After some discussion and clarification, both were willing to try. While it wasn't easy for either of them since a desire for control had been at the center of their conflict, they persevered. They began to understand the other's viewpoint and realize that making sex a contest to see who would win was harming their marriage.

While a sexual fast is an effective tool in creating affection in your marriage, it's not the only or the final solution. It's just one of the many steps toward intimacy presented in this book. If you do embrace the sexual fast, you'll likely find yourself not only leaving mediocre sex and nonsexual affection starvation behind, but you'll also discover your overall relationship beginning to move closer to the extraordinary!

Chapter 13

STARVED FOR
A SHARED VISION

What is a *vision* anyway? A vision is a vivid picture of a desirable future—imagine getting on your tiptoes and looking over the reality of this moment and seeing something out there that doesn't presently exist but is very attractive to you.

We can have a vision for our marriage, our work, and our relationship with our kids. People who accomplish things tend to be vision-driven. They look beyond the details, the minutia, and the problems of the moment in order to see a desirable future.

As the founding fathers of this great nation stood in Independence Hall in 1776, they had a vision. It was an idea, and they wrote down what they believed that idea to be. All of us have been beneficiaries of that great idea, haven't we?

Some people are vision-oriented all the time. God has planted within them a personality where they're constantly looking to the future. I think God has given that gift to me—to be able to look over the top of the current hill and see what's out there. But I've come to the conclusion that not everyone thinks that way. Having a vision isn't something that comes naturally to many of us.

I'm married to a woman whose focus is more immediate than on the future. Donna's primary approach is problem solving for today while I tend to look ahead. In our marriage, we've got to be able to look beyond this moment and see into the future even if having a vision doesn't come naturally to Donna.

When Donna and I got married, I was nineteen and she was eighteen. Our vision at that point was to get to our honeymoon and that was about it.

Most of us think our vision is the next step—say, getting an education. Then getting a job and then a spouse (maybe in reverse order), a home, children, getting children out of the home, and then retiring. We live in little segments or short pieces, looking no further ahead than a few weeks, months, or years.

Why is it important for a married couple to look a little bit beyond where we are today and have a vision? Proverbs 29:18 is foundational to this topic. "Where there is no revelation [or without a vision from God], the people cast off restraint." A vision has several benefits.

First, a vision is a restraining force against evil in our life. When we live for the moment, we will die in that moment. Some people are in prison because they lived for the moment without regard to the future. They couldn't see over the hill to anything more than what they were experiencing right then. When we live for the moment with the problems in our marriage, we're going to stay stuck in the problems. A restraining force permits us to look beyond this moment to the vision God has for our marriage, the bigger picture beyond the issues we're dealing with right now. Seeing the bigger picture can help us work through problems because our goal is a long-term, successful marriage.

I'm convinced that many divorces are the culmination of multiple evils piled one on top of another in a relationship. Most of the time, a couple who has gotten to the point of divorce didn't get there overnight. Rather, a whole series of little evil experiences have occurred. Something was said or left unsaid, or there was infidelity. Perhaps they've gone through a process of forgiveness and rebuilding, but then it happens again and again. Soon a pile of evil has developed in the marriage relationship. As the Bible says, "Where there is no revelation [vision from God], the people cast off restraint." Without the ability to look over the hill of hurt and pain and see all the positives that come from a strong, healthy marriage, there is little to hold us back from thoughtless words or deeds toward our spouse.

I believe very strongly that God wants to give us a vision for our marriage to put boundaries on evil and hold it back. A vision gives us something bigger than ourselves and our needs to focus on.

Second, a vision is a map to the future. As couples, we need to make a plan that will get us to the future together.

The most precious times Donna and I have spent in our thirty-something years together have not been when we've been caught in the minutia of the moment with some problem—like getting our kids to bed at night, or trying to help them get their homework done, or deciding how we're going to pay the bills. The most precious times have occurred when Donna and I have gotten away together, held hands, and walked through Sabino Canyon near our home in Tucson, talking about our life—answering questions like *How are you doing? Where are we headed? Where do you think we should go? What do you think we should be doing? What are we doing right? What are we doing wrong?*

When Donna and I first married back in the early seventies, we spent ten days in California at the training center of Clyde Narramore, a psychologist who is considered one of the founding fathers of Christian psychology. We still consider those as precious days because we were forced into a situation where we had to talk about our life, our upbringing, our personality, areas where we would clash, and things we could do to make our marriage better.

That time helped give us a clearer vision into the future for a lifelong marriage. Through the process of looking ahead, you can also find that same vision. Ask God to give you a map, a vision that will help keep you on track.

Third, a vision is a pathway for navigating through difficult times. Difficulties will come to every marriage, and we see statistically that divorce rates rise for those experiencing hardships in their marriage. A child's illness, a financial reversal, or a health problem can lead to divorce if the couple has not bonded at a level beyond the current problem.

If you're going through a difficulty in your marriage or in your life today, can you look beyond it to see something bigger and better? Can you say, "We're going to make it, honey, because we've got a vision out there to keep moving to this next stage of what God wants for us"? A vision provides a pathway through times of struggle.

Fourth, a vision is a boost to intimacy. If nothing more, it increases communication because you've got to talk about something more than the current problem. You need to answer questions like, *Where are we going to be in a year? in five years? Where do we want to go?* Having a vision increases communication, which increases intimacy in the relationship.

When a couple has a shared picture of the future they want to create for their family, they become closer because they unite to achieve these goals. Vision involves hope. It takes you beyond today to the time when you have accomplished goals and your family has reaped the benefits of your future thinking.

It doesn't mean that we ignore today because we're riveted on tomorrow. But it does involve having a future picture in mind and steering our marriage and family toward that picture of a future state. Your vision for your marriage and family stretches across all levels of intimacy: physical, spiritual, emotional, and relational.

Dave and Patty developed a sense of a shared vision when they did some goal-setting together. Their adult Sunday school teacher had talked about the value of shared goals for a couple, and the two decided to spend a couple of evenings after the kids were in bed in coming up with some goals they had for their family. The specific goals painted a picture of a desirable future condition they hoped to attain.

Each made a list of his or her own goals for the family before they talked about shared goals. Patty wanted all four of their children to walk with God and be active in their church's youth activities. She wanted all to excel in school and have another activity at which each could experience some success, whether it was sports, music, art, or another endeavor. She also hoped to return to nursing when the children were old enough to permit at least a part-time work schedule.

Dave had a specific financial goal he believed he needed to earn in order to provide for his family's immediate and future needs, including college for the children and the couple's future retirement. He, too, longed for the family to be a Christian family where biblical principles were lived out. He wanted time away for him and Patty at least twice a year.

When they compared their lists, Dave and Patty were pleased that there was so much common ground between them. Of course, there were differences, as there are between any two people, but the goals they shared were plenty to give them a vision of a desired future for their family.

They agreed that they would like to see each child receive Christ by the time he or she completed middle school and continue to walk with God as she grew up. Part of their vision as parents was that all four children would attain (or at least be offered the opportunity to attain) college degrees. They agreed that both Dave and Patty had professional goals that they would like to be able to pursue, later in Patty's case. And they foresaw a happy marriage in their desirable future picture. As they continued to talk about their goals and visions over the coming weeks, both realized that family missions trips were a short-term goal they wanted for their family. By writing down their goals and then talking about them and their vision for the future, they were able to begin to plan for the things they wanted to accomplish.

It's possible to connect with another person on a spiritual level and never have physical intimacy or even emotional intimacy with him or her. Many people have intimacy only on the physical level, behaving promiscuously. They may have great sex, but they have no bond at the soul or the spiritual levels. If part of your vision is to increase intimacy at all levels, it will be easier to identify specific steps toward achieving that intimacy. If you want to improve your spiritual intimacy, perhaps you could start studying the Bible together. If you're working on emotional intimacy, you could schedule specific periods of time each week to share your thoughts and feelings with your spouse.

CASTING A VISION

A vision for your marriage should be a vivid picture of a desirable intimate future. Some of us who grew up back in the sixties and seventies feel like today people just want it *now*. But in the heart and mind of everyone is a longing to have something desirable in the future. In the Christian community especially, we should focus clearly on developing a strong, bright, desirable, intimate future for ourselves in our marriages and our other relationships because a bright future gives hope to those around us. As believers in God and his plan for our life, spreading hope is another way of telling others about God and the wonderful things he can do in our life. Our ultimate hope is in the return of Christ, and living well until that day, which honors God and attracts others to him.

What is a great vision? First, **a great vision is bright and distinct.** Think of it as a vivid photograph of what is out there in the future that is desirable to you.

When you sit with your spouse and you talk about your future, use colorful terms to describe what could happen in your relationship spiritually if you really follow God, if you serve him in ways you have never done before.

After my dad had become a successful businessman in Detroit, we lived in a suburb with a nice home, nice cars, and everything we needed for a comfortable life. But at age fifty-three my dad said, "If I continue on this course, in ten more years I'm going to be dead. There's got to be more." As a young teenager, I could hear him talking to my mother about his desire for a future. He sold everything we owned, moved out onto a farmer's field in Michigan, bought a mobile home, and started a camp to help kids. People thought he was crazy. I thought he was crazy. But he had a vision beyond what we were living at the moment, and I could see in my dad's eyes that it was a turning point for him. He didn't want to be making money for this company any longer and just live the corporate dream; he wanted to invest his life in helping kids. That was the birth of Youth Haven Ranches in Michigan and Arizona, where thousands of kids are still being helped today.

My mother and father's vision has carried on through the generations of my own family. My brother Larry and his wife, Cheri, helped cofound the ranch and now run it. My daughter served as a lifeguard at Youth Haven, and several of Dad's other grandchildren have been involved there as well. That bright, vivid picture is an exciting thing. I can still hear my dad describe the camp as he pictured it. If God gives us a vision, he will make it bright and distinct.

Some of us are living at such a low intimacy level in our marriage that we just try to get by, never asking, *God, what do you have for us? How can we develop spiritual intimacy? How can I connect with my mate in a way we've never connected before?*

A vision doesn't occur for the believer who's walking down the street and all of a sudden is struck by this great idea. It has to be planted there by God. Ask God for a vision for your marriage. And when you see it, focus on it until it becomes bright, distinct, and clear.

What are the components of a shared vision? The key ingredients are **a shared purpose, a shared commitment or responsibility, and a shared problem or goal.** Even if you can identify only one of these, you can begin to build a successful future vision.

A shared purpose means you have answered the question, *Why are we here?* If you believe this life is all there is and when you die, you're finished, you'll get all you can out of life with little regard to the future.

But if you realize your purpose is to serve God and serve others, and that eternity awaits you after death, you have a totally different reason to get out of bed every morning. So in order to develop a great picture of the future for your marriage, you need to nail down the purpose you and your spouse share for your marriage.

Michelle and her husband, Sam, lacked a shared purpose in the early years of their marriage. She told me their marriage had been explosive and volatile back then.

She said, "I used to throw things at Sam and chase him through the house trying to get him to talk to me. When we were first married, we moved to where his job was and I didn't have any friends. My husband is supercompetent and analytical, but I doubted if I'd ever get a hug again from him as long as I lived. I didn't want to divorce and we had a child, but I thought I'd never have someone look into my eyes again.

"I was miserable and I begged God to help me. I told him, 'Whatever you tell me to do, I'll do it.' And that was the beginning for me and I know God must have been working in Sam's heart, too. That was the beginning of change in our marriage.

"Sometimes I think of marriage as a boat where two people are fighting over the oars and the boat is going around in circles, not going anywhere. If you follow your husband, like following in a dance or letting him do the rowing, you become a helper and things go much better. My husband cannot lead the family anywhere without me praying for him, supporting him, and believing in him. Working together as husband and wife means there is an order to things, and God will lead my husband's heart.

"One of the best things I can give him is to be happy with what he provides and with the emotional reserves he has to share with me. I pray for him and for his work and try to think the best of him. We're united in where we're going as a couple and as a family. Now we're considering going to missionary training school and completely changing the direction of our life."

When a husband and wife both have faith in Christ and try to obey him and make his priorities their own, they will have a shared purpose for their lives, their marriage, and their family.

Maybe you don't have a shared purpose. If that's the case, do you share a commitment or a responsibility? If you're married, you have a shared commitment. Do you have children? If you do, then you have a shared responsibility. Even if you're married to an unbeliever, you are committed and responsible to the marriage. In fact, the Bible says if you're married to an unbeliever and they're willing to stay with you, stay with him or her (1 Corinthians 7:13).

So if your spouse is not a believer, but you are both committed to raising great kids, that's a commitment you can work on. That's a commitment that can lead to discussions of a shared purpose. Looking together at your children's futures will take you out beyond today where you can begin to agree on what your family's future should look like.

By focusing on areas you agree on and care about, you can begin to look at and talk about the picture of tomorrow that you both want.

You might have a shared problem or a shared goal you need to focus on as a couple. You can work together to solve the problem.

Andy and Lynn had two children nearing college age and no savings. Both parents had jobs, but there never seemed to be enough money to set aside for college. It was all they could do to pay the mortgage and other bills and provide for their children and themselves. Both children were above-average students, but not valedictorians. Andy and Lynn spent countless hours analyzing ways to reduce the family's expenses and finally came up with a plan to finance their children's educations. As a result, they grew closer. They tackled a daunting problem, and after many hours of working together, using a combination of loans, grants, scholarships, and side jobs came up with a plan to help finance the children's educations.

DEVELOPING THE PICTURE

It's wonderful if you share a purpose, responsibilities, and goals, but it doesn't always happen. If you have even one shared area—and certainly nearly every couple can at least come up with a *problem* they share—you can build a brighter future vision for your marriage.

As you develop the picture of your marital vision, make sure that you have the right background setting for the picture. When you take a photograph, you choose where to take it and what will be in the background. The background for setting your vision is the context of your life today, taking into account your strengths, weaknesses, and resources to help you make your vision realistic and reasonable.

While the background is important, it's not the most important thing. Even more critical is making sure both of you are in the picture. The people in the picture are the most important. When you get your photographs back from the drugstore and look at them, what's the first thing you look for? Yourself! If you're not in the picture, you're not as interested.

How do you feel when people show you slides of their visit to the Grand Canyon or Yellowstone, and you see them standing there? You're not all that interested because you're not in the picture. We've got a lot of marriages where one spouse is not in the picture. The husband is in the picture but the wife isn't. Or one person is blurry and the other is in focus.

When we get photographs back, Donna goes through them and suddenly drops one on the floor. I say, "You don't throw pictures away—that's history." But she throws away the ones she doesn't like of herself so no one will ever see them.

In order to cast a vision for your marriage, you both need to be in the picture and it needs to be one worth framing. Make the vision of your marriage such an interesting, vivid, bright picture that you put it on the wall. In fact, if you're a visual type of person, you may want to do just that.

Our board of directors went through a three-day exercise with an outside consultant where we clarified the vision for our ministry. The consultant started with a little exercise that I first thought was rather juvenile. I thought, *We've got all these high-powered people on the board, and we're sitting around doing this silly thing.* Then it dawned on me that we were communicating at the level of what's really important. The consultant asked us to break into groups of four or five and draw a picture of our ministry on an easel. It forced us to really think. One person drew the globe and then someone put a cross in it, and someone else put in a radio microphone. People kept adding to it and after about an hour and a half, we had a picture that represented our hearts' desire for the ministry.

The consultant pointed out what *wasn't* in the picture, parts of the ministry we hadn't included. There may be things in your marriage that are really not part of your vision but you're doing them every day. Maybe you need to stop doing those things and really focus on what is most important.

With your spouse, stand at an easel and say, "Let's draw our marriage. What do we want in this picture? Do we have kids in this picture? Do we have retirement in this picture? Do we have money in this picture? Do we have parents in this picture? Are we going to live here in this picture? Where does God fit into this picture?"

A vision is nothing more than seeing what is in our mind, what we see as a desirable future. Your vision may change over time. But keep asking God, *What do you have for us as a couple? What's in our picture, and what should be taken out?*

Once you and your spouse can stand together on your tiptoes, looking out toward that bright future you desire together, you will have a stronger foundation on which to build a solid marriage. Knowing where you want to go will help you get there as a couple and as a family.

Chapter 14

STARVED FOR SPIRITUAL AFFECTION

Are you and your spouse spiritually united or spiritually fractured? Spiritual oneness is something we should seek, not only with our spouse, but also with other people.

We live in a nation split into groups. In our pluralistic society, some people believe that homosexuality should be accepted. Others believe we should be more involved in human rights around the world, and still others want us to be isolationists. These and other differing views create division.

Unfortunately, spiritual division separates spouses as well. We think if we pray, read God's Word, and go to church together, we have spiritual oneness. But it doesn't happen that way in most relationships.

Often the spiritual element in a marriage gets crowded out as pressures to earn money, balance the budget, maintain a home, and educate the children take precedence.

But spiritual oneness must be nurtured because it enables and completes all other types of intimacy between a man and his wife; it also provides the basis for a shared vision that we talked about in the last chapter. Spiritual unity provides a bedrock of values that can see us through the most difficult marital storms. When both individuals long to please God, values and goals are much more likely to coincide. And couples who share spiritual oneness can take even the most troubling problems to God in prayer and turn to the Bible for answers.

SOUL CONNECTION

Throughout Scripture, human beings bonded at the level of thought and emotion.

One of many biblical stories of soul intimacy is found in the book of Ruth where a deep soul connection occurred between Ruth and Naomi.

Naomi was a Jewess whose sons had married Moabite women, one of whom was Ruth. When Naomi's husband and sons died, she decided to return to her people and she sent her daughters-in-law back to their people in Moab. But Ruth stayed with her mother-in-law, speaking her well-known words in Ruth 1:16, "Wherever you go, I will go; and wherever you lodge, I will lodge; your people shall be my people, and your God, my God." She joined with Naomi in faith, leaving her parents and her people and believing in the God of the Jews.

Married couples with a deep spiritual connection like Naomi and Ruth have the strength in their relationship to withstand the battering of trial and trouble and make it through still united.

Another example of soul intimacy is the story of the love and respect the apostle Paul had for the servant Onesimus in the book of Philemon.

Onesimus was the slave of Philemon, a wealthy man in the church in Colosse. Onesimus ran away from his master, fled to Rome, and met Paul, who led him to Christ. Paul convinced Onesimus to return to Philemon and wrote to Philemon to effect a reconciliation between the two men. Paul and Onesimus held each other in great respect and love, and both of them made difficult decisions to try to do what was right, based on their bond in Christ. Their spiritual intimacy gave them a basis from which to act courageously. Married couples who share this kind of intimacy have a foundation from which to make the hard decisions and carry them out.

The soul is the seat of our emotions and intellect, where we relate to God and others. Part of it is the personality that will go with us into eternity. The Bible says that in eternity we will know as we are known (1 Corinthians 13:12). Our personality is very resistant to change after an early age except through either a very traumatic event or through a "religious conversion." Yet when a person becomes a believer in Jesus Christ, even the deepest part of who he is—the personality—is affected. The way we view life and other people is fundamentally changed.

Spiritual intimacy makes becoming soul mates, which we'll discuss in the last chapter of this book, much more likely and doable. Soul mates are very close emotionally and intellectually. If they have the spiritual connection as well, soulmating takes place on a deeper level. Not only are we close in our thoughts and feelings, but we share the deepest connection possible, the connection in God.

God wants you to experience spiritual intimacy, along with emotional and physical intimacy in your marriage. Most couples find themselves in one of the following four levels of spiritual intimacy. By looking at these and assessing where you and your spouse are, you can begin to strengthen your spiritual oneness.

Spiritual adversaries

This couple is spiritually at war. You might be married to a person who does not believe as you do, does not love the God you love, and could care less what you believe God is doing in your life. He or she might be openly critical and resistant to your spiritual needs and desires.

If this is your situation, you have several options as to how to respond. One is to try to defend your faith by protecting God from all the arrows and bullets from your spouse. But once you become defensive and say, "I'm right and you're wrong," communication is over. God didn't design us to be in a continually defensive mode.

Another option is to go on the attack, thinking, *I am going to come at you so hard that I'll wear you down spiritually*. This tactic usually drives your spouse further away.

Or you could adopt a "foxhole mentality." Bury your head in the sand, hide out, and let the bombs explode around you spiritually. That doesn't accomplish anything either. God does not intend for us to hide out spiritually, thinking, *Because my spouse is a "jerk" spiritually, I don't have to be emotionally or physically intimate with him or her*.

Being spiritual adversaries filters down into every other area of marriage because spiritual oneness is the core foundation for intimacy in marriage. Your children will also suffer from the confusion and hurt they experience.

Spiritual problems can negatively affect the sexual and emotional relationship between husband and wife because we are spiritual, emotional, and physical beings. If our spiritual life is out of whack, that will filter down into the sexual and emotional areas. If you are not able to share spiritual intimacy with your spouse, it is less likely that you will be able to freely give and receive either sexually or emotionally. Your spouse may have a different perspective, values, or views about sex, even views that offend you. Or perhaps he has a poor self-image without knowing how much Christ loves him. We are created in God's image and that gives us the freedom and openness to be able to express ourselves sexually in marriage. But if we don't know Christ and struggle with why we are here and who we are, we may view ourselves as nothing more than animals, lacking that healthy sense of being able to sexually and emotionally express ourselves.

Clearly, if you are spiritual adversaries, you won't have spiritual intimacy, which is at the core of a good marriage. Oneness comes from the spiritual foundation. If we have oneness at this core area of life, the other areas can be worked on.

First Peter 3:1 speaks to the believer married to a nonbeliever, and it says, in this Carlson paraphrase, "Shut up! Back off! Live before your spouse in such a way that he sees Christ in you and it is so appealing he'll be attracted to God." That's what I recommend spouses married to nonbelievers do: Give them some space. Continue to ask God to soften your spouse's heart, but stop nagging your husband or wife.

Spiritual tolerance
Spiritually tolerant spouses are unwilling to understand their spouse's spiritual needs and desires—but they are not resistant to them. Their attitude says, "If you want to be a 'nut case' and hang out with those nuts at church, feel free to do so. It's stupid to me. If you want to take the kids to church, that's fine with me. If you want to give a little bit to church, that's fine. I'm not going to resist you or fight you, but I'm not going to bother to try and understand why this is important to you either. Because it makes no sense to me!" They think it's another phase in your life that will eventually pass.

But a spiritually tolerant spouse is watching you with a critical eye, waiting for you to fall or drop the ball. He is waiting for that next report of a pastor or priest arrested for molesting children, or for a scandal in the church. Then he can say, "See? Religion doesn't work, and God doesn't work." You might feel like you have to measure up or be perfect. You can't yell at the kids or he'd say, "You are not so spiritual because if you were you wouldn't do that."

Unfortunately, the situation is also confusing for the kids. The message is, "Religion is good enough for Mom (or Dad), but I don't buy it! You kids can decide for yourselves when you grow up."

You may feel loneliness and emptiness from this type of marriage. There is danger in this situation. If you are married to a person who doesn't share this need in your life and someone at church says, "Can I pray with you about that?" suddenly you have an emotional response, thinking, *Here is a person who cares about me spiritually.* We need to protect ourselves if we are not spiritually one with our mate because where we are not intimate with our spouse—emotionally, physically, or spiritually— we are vulnerable.

Affairs don't begin overnight, but rather when two people meet each other's needs at one of these levels. I know godly people who have connected with another godly person at the spiritual level. It started in prayer and shared values with no intention of sexual intimacy. But over time, as the need for spiritual intimacy was met by this other person, the conversation suddenly went into their emotional life, the life of the soul.

I've heard people say, "I never had a person who met my needs spiritually, who could pray with me and listen to me and share my values." Before you know it, these two people have moved from spiritual and emotional intimacy to physical intimacy. It began at the spiritual level, and it happens in our Christian churches. It's extremely important to be on your guard about relating to another Christian on a one-to-one basis who is a person of the opposite sex. Whether you're praying together or discussing next week's Sunday school lesson, being alone with someone who has the potential to meet your spiritual and emotional needs is dangerous.

Spiritual cooperation

This is a marriage of mutual respect with a willingness to understand a spouse's spiritual needs and desires and also to express one's own views. "We have shared values, and we both believe in God. Because I love you, I want to know what you believe and why."

But there's a difference between being comfortable spiritually and truly being one. Many people at this level are either spiritually immature or spiritually wrong. They may be involved in cults or in no religion at all, but they consider themselves spiritual. If you were to ask them if they are spiritually united as a couple, they would say, "Absolutely." But we can be spiritually comfortable and cooperative without it having any impact on our life. Unless you both believe that God's Word is the final authority, there will be spiritual chaos in your relationship.

Jeff and Marcie were not Christians when they married. Two years into the marriage, Jeff gave his life to Christ after attending a Bible study at work. Marcie considered herself a spiritual person, and she was a voracious reader about world religions, religious leaders, and others' "experiences with God." As a new Christian, Jeff thought Marcie was interested in the same God he was, but when her interests moved more and more toward beliefs and practices that Jeff was quite sure were not in the Bible—practices involving the use of incense and incantation—he realized that they were not unified in their beliefs. He knew he had to talk seriously to Marcie and try to show her what the Bible said about some of the religions she was interested in. He invited her to a couples Bible study he had heard about in their neighborhood and, together, they grew in their knowledge and understanding of the one true God.

Spiritual oneness

This is the spiritual intimacy that God designed married couples to have—two people who are willing to share their needs, desires, and beliefs, and are committed to mutual spiritual growth and closeness. They stand together on God's Word, looking to him for guidance for their marriage and family.

Besides going to church, this couple discusses what they hear at church. They read the Bible together and when their reading conflicts with a speaker they heard on the radio or even at church, they talk it over, pray about it, even talking to their pastor about it, if necessary. They read books by other Christian thinkers and stay abreast of the issues facing the church. They engage their children in discussions of the tough questions that all believers face at some time in their lives, questions like why God permits evil in the world and will babies who die go to heaven.

The spiritually one couple strives to obey 2 Timothy 2:15 (NASB), "Be diligent to present yourself approved to God as a workman who does not need to be ashamed, handling accurately the word of truth."

If you and your spouse are spiritually unified, understand that you are in the minority. You may share the same desire for unity in Christ; you are able to pray about everything in your life. But it's easy to coast, saying, "Hey, everything's cool here; God's doing the work." You roll along and suddenly some of your spouse's needs start to change, but you don't notice. In business, when everything is going well, you need to watch out because there is usually a problem right around the corner. The same situation can happen in marriage. So don't take spiritual oneness for granted. Also, spiritually unified couples are all different. Don't look at your pastor and his wife and think, *We must not be spiritually one because we don't do things like they do.*

Some couples pray and study the Bible together, and others do that individually. Donna is a private person. She enjoys having private devotions, reading the Bible, or praying alone. She doesn't ever say, "Oh, Randy can we spend the next hour and a half in prayer together?" That's not Donna's heart. Our times of spiritual sharing are an added part of our life as a couple.

But maybe your spouse has a need to spend more time with you spiritually, praying and reading the Bible together often. So don't look at Randy and Donna Carlson or at your pastor and his wife or somebody in your Sunday school and say, "There's the model for what a spiritually one couple looks like!" What matters is the needs of you and your spouse and how you can meet them together. There is no cookie cutter look of a couple that is spiritually one.

It's very important to realize that spiritual unity is not a replacement for emotional or physical intimacy. It is only one-third of the equation. Some couples think spiritual unity is enough to keep them from having emotional and/or physical intimacy in their marriage, but they are wrong. Sometimes a spouse is so involved in the church that there is nothing left for his or her spouse. They have nothing to talk about unless it involves God, and the spouse who is not involved with the church feels like this spiritual spouse couldn't care less about her emotional or physical needs.

Spiritual oneness doesn't necessarily mean spiritual maturity. I mentioned earlier that you can be one and be totally wrong if your unity is not based on God's Word. Sit down together and reevaluate the foundation of your spiritual oneness.

HOW TO GET THERE

For those who have not reached the level of spiritual unity, there is much hope. I often hear statements like, "I wish my husband would be the leader in our family" or "I wish we could go to church together" or "I wish my spouse wouldn't fight me on some of the values we want to teach our children." If you are spiritual adversaries or you are just spiritually tolerating each other or cooperating with each other without this sense of oneness, remember that it's not your job to change your spouse—it's God's responsibility. Many times those who are growing spiritually see their immature spouse and think, *Why doesn't he get with it?* And a barrier immediately goes up in the relationship. It's hard not to want your spouse to be spiritually mature or to be a Christian. Your heart aches for him or her. You want your spouse to experience what God has done in your life, so you lasso him and start dragging him toward spiritual maturity, effectively pushing him further away in the process.

But we must remember that we came to Christ because of our need; we grew because that was the desire of our heart—without coercion from anyone else. And you can't force your spouse to deepen her relationship with God either. It's hard to back off, but it's got to be done.

As I mentioned earlier, one of the most frequent comments I hear from women is, "I wish my husband would be the spiritual leader in our family." I always ask, "How do you define a leader?" Many husbands have no clue what they're supposed to be doing. They feel inadequate and unable to meet your expectations. Perhaps your husband's leadership has been criticized—he read the wrong Scripture, prayed the wrong prayer, had devotions at the wrong time. He might feel like no matter what he does, it isn't good enough.

I'd like to encourage wives whose husbands show a glimmer of leadership to jump all over it and encourage him with, "Thank you, I appreciate that." And then back off and be quiet. Encourage his leadership. Sometimes a wife waits for her husband to be a spiritual leader and when he doesn't lead, she sits back angry, resentful, and bitter. But your marriage and your kids will pay for this attitude. I compare this situation with a plane flying across the country when the pilot has a heart attack and falls on the floor. I hope the copilot knows how to fly that plane. If you have a leader-husband who doesn't have a clue, then you'd better fly the plane, teaching your kids spiritual truths and being the spiritual leader. If you don't have a leader, serve as the leader yourself.

I once heard a pastor make a statement I've never forgotten. He said, "One Christian in a marriage makes it a Christian family." If your spouse isn't a believer, you have to do your job and be the leader. God will bless you and your family because you are doing the right thing, showing your children how a Christian lives even in a difficult situation.

A crucial point is that God's Word is very clear: If you live with a person who is not a Christian or is not growing spiritually, that *is not* grounds for divorce. We read in 1 Corinthians 7:13 (NIV), "If a woman has a husband who is not a believer and he is willing to live with her, she must not divorce him." I'm not talking about abuse or unfaithfulness. You are not to serve as a doormat. But if you're married to a nonbeliever, you have no business being bitter or angry, or divorcing that person. That loophole has been plugged . . . God wants us to stay.

Remember that your faith is based on your relationship with

Jesus Christ, and *you* are responsible for cultivating that relationship. Don't expect your spouse to meet your spiritual needs or make you more spiritual. Often when we go through times of struggle, we are driven closer to Christ as we depend on him.

STEPS TOWARD SPIRITUAL CLOSENESS IF YOUR SPOUSE IS NOT A BELIEVER

If you are a believer but your spouse is not, here are some ways you can move toward spiritual closeness:

1. *Focus on the big picture*—it's not over until we arrive in heaven! God will work in your life through the difficulties you may have living in a marriage with a spiritually immature or adversarial spouse, so keep the big picture in focus. On those days when you feel like walking out or at least screaming from discouragement, remember that it's not over yet. Tomorrow God may do something you never thought would happen.

2. *Focus on areas of shared intimacy*—find areas of common interest and explore them. If you have areas of emotional intimacy or intellectual intimacy with your spouse, develop them. If he's interested in sports, be interested in sports. If she's interested in crafts, be interested in crafts. If you have children, be interested in the children. Enjoy what you do have together and make the most of it. Don't hold back as if to say, "Hey, when you get spiritual, then I'm going to respond to you."

You may be thinking, *But Randy, you don't understand the jerk I'm married to.* If you're a Christian, your job is to live quietly before your spouse, and love him with the kind of love described in 1 Corinthians 13—patient, kind, and long-suffering. There was something about this person that attracted you. Look for that trait and focus on it with thankfulness. Now that you have made a commitment, it's a matter of finding the positives and building on them. Nagging never won anyone to Christ, but love can do it.

3. *Honor your marriage by honoring your spouse.* That means refraining from gossip. Don't tell your Christian friends you want them to pray for your unsaved, heathen spouse and tell them all the bad things he or she does. Asking for prayer for the salvation of your spouse is one thing, but describing his faults is dishonoring him, as is implying to your children that Dad is less of a good man because he doesn't go to church or pray.

To the contrary, if you don't have spiritual oneness in your marriage, you need to make extra efforts to build up your spouse with comments like, "I'm so proud of your dad—look how hard he works" or "I'm so proud of your mom—look how she takes care of you." By showing your children that you love your spouse, even while you are concerned for his spiritual well-being, you honor him, as God requires. Perhaps one Sunday instead of going to church you stay home and say, "This morning I'm going to stay home so I can spend some time with you!" WOW! The message that your spouse is still important to you could impact him even more than a morning in church could. By living your faith and showing your spouse how important he is, you're pleasing God.

4. *Don't focus on the pain.* It's tempting to concentrate on the one area of your marriage that's lacking, particularly if it's the physical, emotional, or spiritual—the big three. Other areas that might present barriers could be financial, recreational, or intellectual differences. You may feel angry at yourself because you got into this marriage and you concentrate on the bad instead of saying, "Other parts of my life are really very good!" By getting your focus off the pain, you can put your situation into perspective.

Every barrier between you and your spouse that you can remove will make intimacy more likely. If you have financial barriers, physical barriers, emotional barriers, or spiritual barriers, deal with them. Do what you can to tear them down.

Then ask God to help you and your spouse move toward spiritual oneness, whether you are spiritually battling, tolerant, or cooperative. He can do what we cannot, and he responds to prayer.

Chapter 15

STARVED FOR TRUST

I'm sure you can remember your wedding day and the joy and hope you experienced on that occasion. Perhaps you're thinking, *That was a long time ago and things are sure different now*. But you made some extremely important promises that day—promises that, if broken, can sound the death knell for your marriage and bring affection starvation to your relationship as well. It's very difficult to experience the richness of affection with someone who has violated your trust.

In this chapter we're going to talk about why keeping these vows or renewing these vows if they have been broken is absolutely critical if you are to have an affection-rich marriage. It's crucial even if you don't want to and you're tempted to throw in the towel.

When Donna and I married as teenagers, we didn't realize the profound truth and the weighty significance of the statement during the ceremony that "marriage shouldn't be entered into lightly." We both thought we understood what love was, but it's taken thirty-three years of marriage to even begin to scratch the surface of what marital love really means and how critical the vows we took that day are even today.

Couples today often write their own vows, but generally

they include the basic commitments we've often heard from the traditional vows:

We gather here today to unite this man and this woman in the bonds of holy matrimony, which is an honorable estate. Into this, these two now come to be joined. If anyone present can show just and legal cause why they may not be joined, let them speak now or forever hold their peace.

Sir, will you have this woman as your lawful wedded wife, to live together in the estate of matrimony? Will you love her, honor her, comfort her, and keep her in sickness and in health; forsaking all others, be true to her as long as you both shall live? (I will).

Will you have this man as your lawful wedded husband, to live together in the estate of matrimony? Will you love him, honor him, comfort him, and keep him in sickness and in health; forsaking all others, being true to him as long as you both shall live? (I will).

These are powerful, life-changing words for any person who truly means them.

Keeping these vows is essential if you're to experience a life of marital happiness, contentment, and joy. Breaking these vows will absolutely guarantee a life of marital frustration, disappointment, and regret. The bedrock upon which marriage is based is trust, and keeping your vows "as long as you both shall live" allows spouses to continue to trust each other. Even one slip can mess things up.

Consider the powerful commitment a man and woman make on the day they marry. The man looks into the eyes of his bride-to-be and, instead of thinking, *I can ruin your life in the next two months*, he honestly and genuinely believes he will:

- love her
- honor her
- comfort her
- keep her in sickness and health
- forsake all others
- be true to her alone

The woman likewise responds from the depth of her heart and promises to:

- love him
- honor him
- comfort him
- keep him in sickness and health
- forsake all others
- be true to him alone

On our wedding day, I was just happy to get through the ceremony without throwing up or fainting and, frankly, I didn't pay as much attention to the significance of what I was saying as I should have. I meant it, but living out those vows for a lifetime is a commitment that far exceeds what the average man or woman honestly contemplates on the day that they marry.

If you are starved for affection, you or your spouse has undoubtedly broken at least one of the promises you made on your wedding day, perhaps several. With all my heart, I believe that vow keepers will have a satisfying married life. Conversely, I also believe that a vow breaker will struggle with great frustration, hurt, pain, and disappointment in marriage. Keeping our vows is the only satisfactory approach to maintaining the kind of marriage God designed for a man and woman to have.

HOW DO WE BREAK OUR VOWS? LET ME COUNT THE WAYS . . .

Unfortunately, if we're honest, most of us have broken our vows at least a time or two in our marriage. That may be a hard pill to swallow, but it's virtually impossible for two people to live together for a lifetime without at some time being unloving, unthoughtful, or even unfaithful, thereby breaking the promises we made on our wedding day.

You may be thinking that being unfaithful is the Big One, and that's true. But breaking our vows to love and cherish can be devastating to a marriage as well. If we want to have a truly happy, lasting, loving, long-term marital relationship, we have to work hard at keeping our vows in all of these areas. Examples of vowbreaking include:

Failure to love. According to 1 Corinthians 13, love is not just a feeling but it's also an action. It's true that you may not feel loved because of unhealthy neediness, as we talked about in chapter 5, but it can also be true that you don't feel loved because your spouse is failing to love you as God designed. And of course the same could be true for your spouse if he or she feels unloved by you.

A wife will never feel loved if her husband doesn't choose to behave in ways that the Bible says are loving. To refresh your memory, 1 Corinthians 13 says love is patient, kind, not jealous, does not brag, is not arrogant, does not act unbecomingly, does not seek after its own interests, is not provoked, does not take into account a wrong suffered, does not rejoice in unrighteousness but rejoices with the truth, bears all things, believes all things, hopes all things, endures all things, and never fails.

As we've said before, it is up to each spouse to let the other know what kind of behavior shows love to him or her. Some of the biblical characteristics such as kindness are universally understood. But our spouse must be told or shown specifically what behaviors really help us feel loved. Clearly, rudeness and destructive criticism are not loving.

Failure to honor. Some of the obvious ingredients in honoring our spouse include showing respect, recognizing their accomplishments, and acknowledging their contributions to our marriage and family. But again, as with showing love, individuals feel honored in different ways. One person feels honored by words of affirmation; another likes a big "Congratulations" sign in the front yard or the red "You Are Special" plate at his place at the table.

A stay-at-home mom should be acknowledged and appreciated for the good job she's doing as the heart of the family. A husband who works outside the home should be honored for his responsibilities and roles. We honor our spouse by recognizing their gifts, their knowledge and abilities, and their contributions to our life.

When we honor a person, we put his needs above our own. When we honor a guest, we bring out the best silverware and china and cook the best meal we can or take her to the nicest restaurant. We use our best language and we are kind and considerate and thoughtful in planning ahead. When we have something in our home that we honor, we display it for other people to see instead of hiding it away. We don't criticize someone we honor, and our attitude is one of cherishing and protecting him. In these practical ways, we can honor our spouse, just as we honor our parents by showing respect and care, not necessarily by obeying them once we are adults.

In chapter 8 we explained the principle of Reality Respect. We can also honor our spouse by allowing them to face the consequences of their decisions and, at the same time, standing by to encourage them and support them as needed.

Bailing out during times of physical, emotional, or mental sickness. It's often easier to be patient and loving with a person who has a physical illness than with one who has a mental or emotional illness. Illness can put a severe strain on marriage. And while mental illness cannot be used as an excuse for abuse or addiction when Reality Respect should be applied, failure to stand by a suffering spouse can be a form of vow-breaking.

Lack of faithfulness. Whenever we put other things ahead of our spouse—our work, a substance such as alcohol or drugs, or another person—we break our marriage vows. We promised to forsake all others, and that means not putting other things we love ahead of our spouse in importance. Unfaithfulness is also shown through lying, cheating, stealing, pornography, and having affairs—all terribly destructive to marriage.

Thoughtlessness. A thoughtless spouse violates her vows by failing to think of her spouse's needs or by being unaware that some things she says or does are hurtful or annoying—everything from leaving the cap off the toothpaste tube to not helping out around the house. Thoughtlessness is a form of irresponsibility because we are responsible to understand and love our spouse. Thoughtlessness attacks the fabric of our marriage. While a spouse who is caught in an adulterous affair may face swift and direct consequences of that behavior, we often tolerate thoughtlessness for a lifetime, simply burying our emotions or showing thoughtlessness in return. But thoughtlessness is just as destructive as other forms of unfaithfulness.

Failure to comfort. I've observed that, in a way, a man sets the temperature of the family, and a woman sets the temperature of her man. If I've had a good day and I'm up and positive and optimistic, things at home seem to be up and positive and optimistic. On the other hand, if I come home after a very difficult meeting or am feeling discouraged and I bring that attitude home, I can feel the overall energy in my family decrease. Even my dog seems a little frustrated. But when I feel Donna's love and respect in the form of a positive word of encouragement, I feel better. That translates into a more pleasant atmosphere for all of us. Of course, women need comfort, too, because they struggle with many of the same issues men do with work, responsibilities, and relationships. We all need comfort from time to time.

Trust is the foundation of strong relationships, including marriage. When a vow is broken, trust is broken. A relationship based on trust can face almost any problem.

Rate yourself as a vow keeper
Ask yourself these questions:

1. How have I shown honor to my spouse in the past week?
2. During the past twenty-four hours, in what specific ways have I demonstrated love for my spouse?
3. How do I handle the situation when my spouse is ill?
4. Have I allowed anything (another person, work, family, hobbies) to come between my spouse and me?

5. How kind am I to my spouse when I feel mistreated by him or her?
6. Am I holding any resentment or grudges against my spouse?

WHAT ABOUT WHEN YOU'VE BLOWN IT?

We behave our way into becoming a vow breaker, and we can only behave our way into being a vow keeper. Good intentions won't do it. "I'm sorry" won't do it. Flowers and candy won't do it. Only vow-keeping behaviors will do it.

Jason had been cheating on his wife, Amanda, for five years when she learned of it. When he was caught, Jason apologized and promised to break off the relationship. He couldn't understand why Amanda still got upset when he went to bars with his male coworkers since he was no longer seeing the woman with whom he'd had a relationship. Jason needed to learn that saying you're sorry and even ending a relationship doesn't mean trust is instantly restored. Changed behavior over a substantial period of time is what builds trust. Skirting along the edge of what your spouse can live with just won't restore your relationship. You will need to go the extra mile to be sure she can begin to trust you again.

None of us is perfect. We've all said thoughtless words or failed to comfort when our spouse had a bad day. Some of us have failed in major ways like adultery or abuse. The good news is that we can change, if we're willing to seek help, stay accountable, and prioritize making a change in our behavior. It will take time, perhaps lots of time, to rebuild trust if you have been dishonest or disrespectful to your spouse repeatedly. But the time you invest in rebuilding trust will pay off in huge dividends in your marriage and family and for you personally because you will rebuild your self-respect at the same time. Equally essential is being willing to give and receive forgiveness. With time and effort, you can go from being a vow breaker to being a vow keeper.

WHAT ABOUT WHEN YOUR SPOUSE HAS BLOWN IT?

Once lost, trust is hard to regain. It must be earned back. On the other hand, if your spouse has broken one or more vows and honestly repented and stopped the vow-breaking behavior, you need to begin to build that trust again. It's very difficult for a person who is trying to regain trust if he meets suspicion every day when he gets home from work. In the "love chapter," 1 Corinthians 13, we read that love "believes all things" (v. 7). Of course, we don't want to believe lies, and we must deal with vowbreaking by using Reality Respect as discussed in chapter 8. But once the issue has been dealt with, we must trust God to help our spouse keep her promises and help by not mentioning the broken vow again and again.

Chapter 16

STARVED FOR CONTENTMENT

Kayla found contentment in her marriage despite severe adversity. Kayla has had degenerative Parkinson's disease for eight years.

"I used to be concerned because my husband wasn't very demonstrative," she said. "He didn't hold my hand in public or put his arm around me. But in the last eight years, I've seen true love in action. We've just celebrated our twenty-fifth wedding anniversary, and I've learned that love isn't necessarily just holding your hand. It's lifting you up; it's just being there. My husband is my best friend, and he has been for thirty years. We're called to pick up our cross daily, and sometimes I can't carry my cross because there are times when I'm very ill. He picks it up for me every day and works hard and is a good, godly man. There's more to intimacy than physical things, and he gives so much to me. But I wonder about his emotional needs. Are they being met when I'm not able to give to him like I'd like to?"

I told Kayla that the practical things he does for her probably help him feel useful and appreciated. As he provides for her and loves and cares for her, his needs are probably met, too. I said, "And as you go out of your way to do some extra things to let him know how you appreciate him and care for him in ways he understands, he'll know he is loved in return."

She said, "I wish I could make lunch for him again and do little things for him. But he's the one now who is coming home and making dinner after working all day, the one scrubbing the bathroom and sorting socks. The physical problems have just gotten in the way with the medicine and how fast the disease has progressed. It's encouraging to me to know that his serving me is helping him, because I never really thought of it that way."

By meeting each other's needs, doing what needs to be done, and showing appreciation, Kayla and her husband experience closeness, intimacy, and love, despite her illness. The two are content, despite their many difficulties.

In our consumer society, it's hard to feel content. We are made to think we need a newer car, a bigger home, a nicer vacation, more clothes, and a host of other things that cost money. There's never quite "enough" money to provide for ourselves as we'd like there to be.

This lack of contentment spills over into marriage as well. Media portrayals of gorgeous people of both sexes having tons of fun and excitement can make a married couple wonder, *What's wrong with us?*

Let's look at some factors that play into the lack of contentment many people feel.

THEN AND NOW

What I call the Attraction Principle is very important. The Principle says that what originally attracted you to your spouse can hinder your level of contentment later on because you expect to continue to find your spouse attractive in the ways you did before marriage. The Principle has two parts: We must focus on being attracted to our spouse's character more than her physical beauty, and on the flip side, we must try to remain attractive, considerate, clean, and good-smelling for our spouse so she can remain attracted to us.

When I speak at marriage conferences, I often ask the women to tell me what it was that attracted them to their spouses. I typically hear such things as, "He was godly," "He was understanding," or "He was patient." And then I hear things like, "I liked his car," "I liked his hair," or "He was fun to be with."

From the men I usually hear about physical characteristics: the way she looked. That's very stereotypical, but it seems to actually play out that way.

Often, the characteristics that were initially attractive end up being problematic. A man might tell me he was attracted to his wife because she was attractive, outgoing, and a little flirtatious with him. Later in the marriage he might feel like she's not very responsible and she flirts with other men. Or a woman might say what attracted her to her husband was that he was so understanding. Later he seemed to stop being understanding. Being interested and understanding in the dating stage was part of his best behavior he employed to gain her interest in the beginning of their relationship, but now he just sits around, primarily concerned with his own interests. He no longer seems to care about what interests her.

Of course, we all change over time. If attraction is built on characteristics that change over time, like appearance, it can create a problem. Obviously, we change physically. We can get things tucked and pulled and tightened, but the bottom line is the aging process gets all of us, and we need to understand that taking care of ourselves is something we need to continue to work on.

Not only do we need to be attractive for our spouse, but we need to be attracted *to* our spouse. We need to find contentment, and in order to do that we need to keep our expectations in line with reality: Your husband at fifty-five is probably not going to look like he did at twenty-five.

But after marriage, some people don't take care of themselves. I joke about the man who, while they were dating, would shower and smell good, and then after the marriage would come home with greasy hands from work and sit on the couch and pick lint from his belly button—not too attractive to his wife!

We once did a radio program called "Living with a Slob." I thought no one would call in, but our lines were flooded by people who were exasperated about living with a person who had really surprised them by turning into an absolute slob.

Part of the Attraction Principle says we must make a decision to remain physically attractive for our spouse and to continue those attributes they fell in love with in the first place, whether that's understanding, humor, talking together, or sharing interests. By the same token, we need to stay interested in and attracted to our spouse and to have realistic expectations.

As I said earlier, attraction based on changing characteristics is like a house built on shifting sand. Begin to cultivate your appreciation for your spouse's character, a lasting trait that will be there long after the trim waist and the smooth skin are gone. Look for your spouse's strengths in areas like commitment, honesty, hard work, loyalty, kindness, generosity, and loving parenting—and focus on appreciating him and thanking God for him on a daily basis. These durable characteristics are much more valuable than an attractive face or body—so tell your spouse often that you appreciate him.

LOVING ANYWAY . . .

Sometimes contentment in marriage is extremely hard to come by. Listen to Cindy's tragic story:

"After a year of dating when everything seemed all right, we were married. But our marriage has been difficult from the start. My husband turned out to be schizophrenic and manic-depressive, and back then—twelve years ago—we didn't know much about those conditions.

"Imagine yourself as hungry as you can be, and all you can think about is eating. I definitely feel starved for affection—starved and also isolated from others. I sometimes question God and ask *why am I in this situation?* The pain is excruciating.

"It's been hard on my children too. They don't want to bring anyone home because of where we live. The kids have been confused and unhappy, and they don't understand why God doesn't just lift this. They pray that God will heal their dad and he hasn't, so my son turned away from Christ.

"I can't invite people over because I never know what my husband's going to do. He's able to cook for me and he does some things like that. But to me affection would be honesty, trust, stability, respect, and nurturing. I don't know how my husband would define affection. We don't have a sexual relationship because when we try my husband gets some terrible thought or hallucination and it's impossible. We've been in counseling for many years and he has his good days and bad days. I'm learning patience.

"I'm not close to my extended family, but I treasure my friends from church. I can talk openly to them about my problems and ask for prayer and counseling. I study my Bible and pray a lot.

"Having a thankful attitude for the things I do have and helping others takes the sorrow away for a little while. By getting my mind off my own sadness and making someone else smile, I kind of forget what I'm going through. I don't understand what God has for me, so I just go one day at a time. My life and my children's lives are sometimes very difficult, but if I am faithful to God, he will use the difficulty for good somehow in our life."

Cindy's husband has many problems—but she loves him anyway. People have asked me, "Why do I need to love an unlovely spouse?" That's a great question, and the answer is somewhat counterintuitive. If your spouse is difficult, you may feel that you have the right to lash back, make your point, set the record straight, win the fight. You may be justified in human terms for those feelings and your response.

But we must love anyway for several reasons:

1. *God commands us to.* Have you ever thought of your spouse as your greatest enemy? He or she may be when it comes to your peace of mind, contentment, and happiness. Jesus gave us a powerful command for living a Christian life in Luke 6:35, "Love your enemies, do good, and lend, hoping for nothing in return; and your reward will be great, and you will be sons of the Most High . . ." God commands us to love those who are unloving toward us, and we will be rewarded for that kind of love.

2. *It builds our character.* We grow stronger in self-control when we choose not to let our feelings rule our behavior. Instead, we respond in a manner that's consistent with our beliefs.

3. *It's the only hope for restoration.* No matter if you choose a tough-love approach or a soft-love approach, you will only see restoration in your relationship when you choose to focus on dealing with the issue at hand and not lashing back. Every time we respond in kind to an unloving spouse, it puts one more layer of bricks in the wall that will divide your relationship.

4. *It frees us from anger, resentment, and unrealistic expectations, and opens the door to contentment.* The "illusion of change" tells us if we keep hammering away at a spouse, things will change. Instead, she just hides out from the nagging and the

change is just an appearance, not reality. When we love any-way, we are freed from the frustration of seeing nothing change. Real change must come from inside when a person decides she wants something better and different.

She may start wanting something different after experienc-ing a dose of Reality Respect, or natural consequences of her actions and behavior. As we talked about in chapter 8, conse-quences take many forms. A husband might stop calling a wife's office and saying she's sick if she's really been drinking again. A wife might hire a carpenter to repair a broken piece of furniture if her husband won't help out around the house.

Loving someone enough to hold him or her accountable is probably the highest form of love. It is freeing for both the giver and receiver of that love because it ends the power struggle and fosters the contentment that comes with accepting reality and letting consequences do their work.

Cindy's story shows how sometimes even after you've done everything possible, your marriage doesn't get any better. I'd like to talk now about how to survive when nothing works.

Cindy's husband's illness makes their life very hard. But many times, marital misery is caused when a spouse continues to break his or her promises to be loving, kind, and faithful. Ob-viously, it's hard to know what to do in this kind of situation be-cause at this point the marriage is far beyond just being starved for affection. It has reached the point of being starved for sur-vival and very likely will need to be put on spiritual, emotional, and relational life support.

SURVIVING IN A TOUGH SPOT

There are times when, with a pastor's support and counsel, di-vorce is the right thing to do. One woman's daughters were being sexually abused by their father and counseling and confrontation didn't stop the abuse. With the concurrence of both her counselor and her pastor, she filed for divorce to protect her girls from further mistreatment and damage.

I'd like to talk to you, however, about how to survive in a difficult situation if you choose to stay. Three things are crucial for you to do:

1. *Maintain your integrity and self-respect.* Integrity is doing right even when no one is watching; living with integrity will produce self-respect. You need to do the right thing because you have to live with yourself. Integrity involves applying the principles of Reality Respect, knowing that we reap what we sow. Our actions do indeed produce consequences.

2. *Find a trusted mentor, coach, or counselor.* Be careful with friends and family because they are usually too close to the situation and won't be the kind of help you need. They are not unbiased and they have their own slant on the situation. You need someone objective who can ask the hard questions and hold you accountable for decisions you've made. The Scriptures tell us that "two are better than one, because they have a good return for their work" (Ecclesiastes 4:9, NIV). This is not a time to be a lone ranger. You need to find someone who is godly and mature, someone you can talk to, someone who can help you think through the strategies you need to develop. This person can help you strengthen your grip on your emotions and reach out in healthy ways to those who can encourage you. You'll also need to review your expectations so that you're taking reality into account in terms of what your spouse is capable of giving.

3. *Pray regularly and continually.* The prayers of a faithful man or woman will avail much (James 5:16). God loves us and he is the healer of our soul and, I think, of our relationships.

Pray for direction. Pray for your spouse. Pray for yourself. Pray to be a vow keeper, no matter what.

BROKEN VOWS

We talked in chapter 15 about broken vows that are at the heart of most marital desperation. It seems to me that there are different levels of heartache caused by broken vows, and different responses are required.

If your spouse is thoughtless, you often feel hurt and frustrated. Someone married to a thoughtless person feels separated from the person and the two simply coexist. They watch TV together, eat together, raise the kids together, go on vacations together, and have sex. They may be living in the same house, but they're miles apart.

Thoughtlessness and the ensuing lack of attention tend to wear away a marriage like dripping water wears away at a rock. The concern for the well-being of your spouse and for the marriage gradually erodes the foundation of love you started with. One way a person knows she is experiencing this level of vowbreaking is that she feels hurt and frustrated.

If your spouse is unloving, you may feel angry and resentful. Jesus addresses this in Luke 6:32-33 when he says, "But if you love those who love you, what credit is that to you? For even sinners love those who love them. If you do good to those who do good to you, what credit is that to you? For even sinners do the same." He's saying we are to be counterintuitive and countercultural when it comes to responding to unloving people, and that includes our spouse. If we allow the anger we feel toward an unloving spouse to continue, it will affect us emotionally, spiritually, and probably physically as well.

But perhaps most painful of all is when the vow to be

faithful is broken. If your spouse is unfaithful, you feel devastated. In addition to ongoing mentoring, counseling, and Reality Respect, along with a lot of prayer and love, you need to take some strong action. Obviously, if a person wants to divorce or leave the relationship, he will do that. But the focus of this book is to help you survive if you choose to stay in a very difficult situation.

God tells us that the marriage bed is to be kept pure and that we are to remain faithful to each other in our marriage. Anything less is not to be tolerated. This doesn't mean that a person whose spouse has been unfaithful needs to run to an attorney and file for divorce, but she clearly needs to do three things.

- First, she needs to permit herself to have a broken heart, which allows her to feel her pain and deal with it.
- Second, she needs a clear head, which allows her to rise above her emotions and seek help in putting together a strategy for the confrontation necessary in an unfaithful vow-breaking situation.
- Third, she needs strong knees so she can spend a lot of time in prayer on behalf of her marriage.

Todd learned about Gina's unfaithfulness when he confronted her about being out "with her girlfriends" several nights a week, leaving their two children with Todd or a babysitter. When a man had called the house and asked for Gina but wouldn't identify himself, Todd determined to talk to her about it calmly. He told himself she couldn't possibly be seeing someone else because they loved each other very much. The thought of her with another man hurt and angered him. He knew he would need a couple of days to calm down and pray for

God's help, so he waited until the weekend to talk to her. He took a vacation day on Friday, drove to his favorite fishing spot, and begged God to save his marriage.

Gina wept when he asked her about her increasingly frequent absences and the man who had called. She said she was almost relieved that Todd had found out and confronted her. She asked him to go with her to the pastor to try to figure out what to do.

Gina and Todd had a rough road ahead of them to heal the breach that had occurred, but Todd's wise preparation and courage in confronting his wife at least opened the door to healing.

I don't want to present you with "easy believism" that says if you do it God's way, everything will turn out the way we want. He doesn't promise us that everything will turn out the way we want, even if we obey him. What he does promise is that he will work all things together for our good if we love him (Romans 8:28-29), and we can count on him to fulfill that promise. He can provide us with contentment even in the midst of great turmoil and trouble. Our part is to obey him, live with the integrity and self-respect that allows our spouse to experience the natural consequence of his choices, to return good for evil, and to continue to love. God's part is to take a mess and bring good out of it. I've seen him do it; I believe he will do it for you.

Chapter 17

SOULMATING

We've seen that marriages can experience affection starvation in a number of areas. One or both marriage partners can be starved for conversation, tenderness, nonsexual affection, passion, shared vision, spiritual affection, and contentment. We've also looked at some specific ways to feed your marriage in these areas. I hope some of the ideas you've read about have given you new hope and energy with which to revitalize your marriage. I've seen it happen in many marriages, and I believe that your marriage, too, can become one marked by affection and joy.

I'll conclude with one final concept that will be an enduring part of your efforts to improve the affection in your marriage. I like to use the term *SoulMating*, which I use as a verb because SoulMating is something couples *do* with each other. It's a matter of commitment and work for two people to SoulMate, and be warned: It's not an easy process. You must take into account your different backgrounds, experiences, priorities, and ways of relating to life. To make SoulMating successful, it's also vital to maintain a realistic view of the needs and expectations you both have. I'll repeat the equation mentioned in chapter 7: *Expectation minus Reality equals Disappointment*. Both disappointment and disillusionment are inevitable when individuals foolishly believe that SoulMating is finished on the day they marry. The fact is, SoulMating has only begun. It takes a lifetime of emotional, physical, and spiritual exploration before the SoulMating process begins to fully gel.

SoulMating means putting in the time and effort to become a kindred spirit with your spouse, where you relate on a deep level unparalleled in any of your other human relationships.

Here are a few signposts indicating that the SoulMating process is happening:

- You can finish each other's sentences, but you don't.
- You completely understand the meaning of a look without a word being spoken.
- You can read each other's minds, but are still sensitive to confirm your interpretation before doing anything.
- You anticipate your spouse's needs in advance, and you try to meet them.
- You're interested in your partner's thoughts and feelings and enjoy sharing together.
- It's getting easier to put the needs of your spouse and your marriage ahead of your own.
- Thoughts of divorce or fantasies of someone else making you happy are gone.
- You accept your spouse's opinions on faith, money, sex, family, and relationships, and try to cooperate instead of compete.
- You desire to be with your spouse.
- You're closer today than you were yesterday.

As you review these signposts, if you find that many of them simply do not apply to your marriage or, even worse, that just the opposite is true for your relationship, it's never too late to take action and restore your marriage. You can make the difference between having a well-nourished or malnourished relationship with your spouse.

EVERYBODY WANTS ONE

The "soul mate" business has become a huge industry in today's culture. Movies, reality TV shows, and books are being pumped out daily, each selling the sizzle of how complete your life will be when you find the right—perhaps even perfect—person to be your soul mate. It's an easy sell to an affection-starved world.

The Internet offers pages of articles, scores of groups, and tons of businesses that are leveraging the soul-mate wave for all it's worth. These sites brashly claim they can help people find that one and only person for them. One site states they will assist people who are tired of "sifting, sorting, and dating people" they have nothing in common with. It offers a series of tests to take to determine if the chemistry is right with the person you're now with. Another site helps people unearth a serious long-term relationship through a battery of psychological and physiological profiles. It points out that if two people don't match on *all* levels, their relationship just won't work. A third site claims to be *the* dedicated site for those who are on the hunt for their kindred spirit. I could have easily spent a day surfing all the sites available, but my quick sampling told me that people are desperate to find the right person with whom to share their life.

It can be comforting to imagine that somewhere in this wide world there is just *one* person waiting to make *you* happy. Someone who can meet your needs, love as you desire to be loved, and always be there for you. It's a heartwarming picture, but one that's far from true—unless both people are willing to put away their immaturity and each give 110 percent to the marriage in order to make it a success.

You might be thinking I'm one cynical guy, but as a marriage and family therapist I have met many "wannabe" soul mates who have become nothing more than lonely and disappointed "soul*less*" mates. Yet I also know there are husbands and wives who've followed through with the vows they made on their wedding day and continuously nurtured a marriage rich in affection. These are the couples who have learned the secret I'm about to share with you—that a soul mate doesn't just *happen*. Becoming a soul mate takes action!

That's the exact advice I gave Elise. In the two short years since Kevin and Elise had married, the reserve of affection between them had been all but used up. "What scares me the most now is my feelings for Kevin are dying," Elise admitted. "I've become numb. I guess it's my way of self-protection."

I told Elise she needed to do something before her feelings for Kevin completely vanished. I explained how feelings always follow thought and behavior and said she needed to go on a one-person SoulMating crusade.

BECOME *MARRIAGE* FOCUSED

I've already recommended four steps to revitalizing your marriage in chapter 7, after you adjust your expectations to make them realistic and achievable. The four steps were:

1. Study your spouse.
2. Affect your spouse.

3. Communicate with your spouse.

4. Focus on your spouse.

But here I'd like to make a slight modification to these steps by switching the emphasis away from your *spouse* and directing it instead toward your *marriage*. Marriage has a life of its own and needs to be fed and nurtured. It may appear at first glance that I'm only talking about semantics here, but there is a vast difference between a spouse-focused relationship and one that is marriage-focused. The unity candle ceremony provides a good illustration.

The unity candle ceremony involves three candles, one representing the groom, one signifying the bride, and the larger one depicting the new marriage about to be launched. Once the couple ignites the single flame of unity, their individual candles are extinguished. The symbolism is powerful: Two people are now becoming one before God and man.

God didn't intend for you to blow out your individuality when you married, only your independence. *Inter*dependence becomes the new priority, with both people making the marriage the top focus of their lives, above everything except their relationship with Jesus Christ.

Let's talk about expanding the emphasis to also include your marriage.

1. Study your marriage

Step back and take an honest look at what's missing in your relationship. You must be brutally honest with yourself and realize it's not all about your spouse. In fact, you can't change your partner anyway, so this exercise will focus largely on you. When Elise took a hard look at her marriage, she wasn't pleased. Beyond a lack of affection, she was able to identify four other troubled spots: poor communication, an inability to resolve conflicts, in-law problems, and lack of a shared vision.

I asked Elise to consider this question, "What can you do now that would make the greatest improvement in your own life and in the life of your marriage?" She pinpointed four things she knew she could do to make a difference: 1) pray daily for her marriage and for Kevin; 2) locate a counselor who could help her throttle back her explosive temper; 3) take the initiative to discover Kevin's love language; and 4) commit to become a better listener. None of her actions would guarantee that Kevin would instantly change into Mr. Perfect, but they would surely change *her*.

Here are some questions you may want to ask yourself as you study your marriage:

- What can I do to improve communication?
- How do I contribute to a lack of affection?
- When and how did things turn for the worse in the relationship, and how did I contribute to that?
- What can I do in service to my marriage (not just to my spouse)?
- What are the five most important things to me in marriage?
- What are the five most important things to my spouse in marriage?
- If I could wave a magic wand and makes things better, what would be different?

I asked Elise to look at the following lists and tell me which one applied to her marriage. Which one applies to your marriage?

Spouse-Centered

- 🐾 Your spouse's moods can ruin your day.
- 🐾 It's difficult to confront your spouse without feeling afraid.
- 🐾 You tend to ruminate on what your spouse is doing wrong.
- 🐾 It's often difficult for you to respect your spouse.
- 🐾 You fear rejection or abandonment.

Marriage-Centered

- 🐾 You easily rise above your spouse's moods.
- 🐾 You confront problems in your relationship without fear.
- 🐾 You've developed healthy outlets for personal growth.
- 🐾 You haven't lost your individuality, only your independence.
- 🐾 You and your spouse are interdependent and understand your roles in the marriage.

Elise said the spouse-centered marriage was a closer fit for her and Kevin. But a spouse-centered marriage can put too much control in the hands of the unaffectionate, less sensitive person. This was the case for Elise and Kevin. Kevin had become less affectionate than he once was, and the result was an inconsistency that drove Elise nuts: She called it Kevin's "jerkiness." As she allowed his actions to dominate her thoughts, feelings, and behavior, Elise lost her joy and zest for life.

SoulMating couples are marriage-centered. When a relationship becomes marriage focused, both your needs and the needs of your spouse can be fulfilled. If you're like Elise and find yourself in a malnourished marriage and desire to deepen your relationship with your spouse, there are some basic, practical things you can do to turn things around.

2. Affect your marriage

When I say "affect," I'm talking about impacting or influencing your marriage for good. This is tough because it requires humility and courage. Setting aside your own needs, desires, and wants will likely not come without some resistance from within, especially if you believe you've already given about as much as you can to your spouse. Try to remember that you're doing this for your marriage, which means your efforts will ultimately come back as a gift to yourself.

Elise was able to humble herself enough to affect her marriage, and as she did, she saw a positive impact. Elise decided that while she couldn't change Kevin, she could change herself. She asked Kevin to meet her for lunch, at which time she told him how much she loved him and wanted an affectionate marriage. She also said that since she felt like she was too reliant on Kevin's moods and when he felt like showing affection, she was going to develop some healthy outside interests that would help her take the focus off of her need for his attention. She planned to enroll in an art class at the community college in their town.

"I felt like I was doing something productive. My commitment to Kevin increased and I felt hopeful," Elise said. "Kevin was still pretty much the same guy, but I wasn't the same person. The real turning point came when I got my eyes off of Kevin and me and placed them instead on what was best for our marriage." Elise was willing to make something happen, and the results were encouraging.

Here are some basic rules to follow when attempting to affect your marriage:

- Don't try to change your spouse
- Work on one thing at a time
- Maintain realistic expectations
- Remember that your marriage is more likely to change when you change

3. Focus on your marriage

Each time you're tempted to lose patience with your spouse, remember that he's only half of the marriage equation. As you make your marriage the focus of your attention, you'll find it easier to deal with those things about your spouse that bug you. You focus on your marriage by:

- **Not keeping score.** Marriage isn't a contest; it's cooperation, and you may end up carrying more of the emotional, spiritual, and physical load than you had anticipated. But you can either keep working on the process of marriage, or you can get out. I strongly recommend the first option.
- **Going the extra mile.** That may mean confronting a problem even when you don't want to, being silent when you want to speak, or setting a boundary when it would be easier to give in. The deciding question needs to be, "What is the right thing to do for the health of my marriage?" Let me add a caution: If you are in an abusive, alcoholic, or otherwise dangerous marriage, you need to first seek professional help. It's been my experience that the steps I've outlined here can only succeed in a safe environment.

A number of years ago I ran across the following "Rules for a Happy Marriage." Donna and I strive to live by each, and as a result our marriage has grown closer:

1. Never both be angry at once.
2. Never yell at each other . . . unless the house is on fire.
3. Yield to the wishes of the other, even if it's solely as an exercise in self-discipline.
4. If you have a choice between making yourself or your mate look good—choose your mate.
5. If you feel you must criticize, do so lovingly.
6. Never bring up a mistake from the past.
7. Neglect the whole world rather than each other.
8. Never let the day end without saying at least one complimentary thing to your partner.
9. Never meet without an affectionate welcome.
10. Never go to bed mad.
11. When you've made a mistake, talk it out and ask for forgiveness.[9]

AN EMOTIONAL HUG

I've been talking about the steps Elise took to work on her marriage. But what about Kevin? With him, it all boiled down to the same thing it does for most men: showing affection in a way that truly affects their wives.

I've never been what you would call an emotional kind of guy. I'm not touchy-feely, and I don't go around hugging everyone I meet (unless I know the person well or they're family, and even then I want to know if they've had a cold in the last ten days). I don't spill my guts at the drop of a hat or open up quickly with people I don't know well. But I've learned an important lesson about emotions and marriage. You'll never be any closer to your spouse than when you are willing to share your heart, and you give your spouse a big, warm "emotional hug" when you give her the kind of affection that makes her feel closest to you.

Elise hadn't had an "emotional hug" from Kevin since the very start of their marriage. Sure, she had received lots of sexual hugs, but she was starved for a deeper form of intimacy—emotional affection. I told Kevin, "With your hand, heart, and head, you could turn your marriage around in a week." A week? I meant that.

What Elise needed from Kevin was rather basic: from his hand, loving touches without sex; from his heart, tender expressions of concern for her well-being and an understanding ear; and from his head, time together to talk about their future plans. That was it. I explained to Kevin that the choice, quite simply, was his. He could continue experiencing a growing distance from Elise, or he could start loving her the way he promised he would on their wedding day.

Thankfully, Kevin chose to go to work on his marriage, to begin the SoulMating process. Now, both Elise and Kevin were taking the action necessary to restore and reenergize their relationship and to begin becoming soul mates for life.

Elise had started the process alone by facing the reality of their situation and talking to me as a counselor. Fortunately, she didn't wait until years and years of coldness had seeped into her heart, making the rebuilding process more difficult. Her actions led to understanding on Kevin's part and a commitment to work together to change their relationship.

THE RIGHT PERSON

Soul mates know that it's not just about finding the right person.

Some people think soul mates hug, hold, and kiss with intimacy and passion; converse in an interesting and engaging manner anytime day or night; and are fully capable of emoting on demand.

If this is your spouse, congratulations! You've hit the marital jackpot! I'd strongly recommend that you hang on to him or her tight, because you've got a keeper. If I supported cloning, I'd suggest you have your spouse duplicated, packaged, and sold on the Internet . . . being sure, of course, that you keep the original.

Reality, though, manifests itself in the form of flawed human beings like Kevin, who couldn't find an emotional response if he tripped over it. He's the kind of guy who is great with figures, computers, logic, and a number two pencil. But when it comes to vulnerably and genuinely showing his emotions, Kevin's in way over his head. Elise was so hurt by Kevin's coldness that she had convinced herself he had scammed her. She felt that Kevin had lured her with promises of endearment, only to deliver a loveless relationship for both of them. While he was in hot pursuit of Elise, Kevin had mustered up just enough emotional maturity to win her affection. Unfortunately, that facade of maturity quickly faded shortly into the marriage.

It took only two years before Elise started to verbalize her belief that she had fallen victim to a bait and switch. Kevin wasn't the same guy she had married, and Elise was more certain than ever that she had made a big mistake. As she put it, "The chemistry is gone and I need to feel something again." It wasn't that Kevin was guilty of having an affair or had become abusive. Simply, the luster that makes all new husbands look shiny and new had been rubbed away by the realities of life, and Elise wasn't prepared for the tarnished man that she was now seeing. We're all tarnished in one way or another, because no one is perfect.

More important than finding the right person is *being* the right person, which I'd like to distinguish from being *right*. I once heard a man say that behind the success of his marriage was "a willingness to be wrong once in a while." Our humanness screams to be right. From childhood, the need to be right is strong within us. Rightness helps make sense of the world.

On some points, such as faith, values, and certain behaviors, you do need to draw clear lines between right and wrong. It's different, however, in marriage. Do you find yourself needing to be right about things that really don't matter? If you need to be right, it's likely that you'll either argue a point until it's dead without ever giving in, or you'll just walk away from the argument but comfort yourself by saying, "They just don't get it." You may just go away so you can build a case for later debate. But does it really matter?

If you can put aside your need to be right and focus on becoming the right kind of person—a person who is able to be wrong once in a while, a person who can agree to disagree, a person who can apologize when necessary—you'll find that the benefits you experience in your marriage relationship will far outweigh the little victory that comes with being "right" in an argument or discussion.

I can assure you that you have found the right person. At the moment you said, "I do," your spouse became the right person for you—period. There is no place for second thoughts.

DIVORCE IS NOT AN OPTION

Soul mates understand the importance of commitment. The looking is over. The choice has been made. Now it's time to bring chemistry to the marriage.

Can you remember how you felt on your wedding day?

Standing close by, looking into the eyes of your love, rehearsing your lines, hoping not to stumble in front of family, friends, and God. As you peered into the soul of lifetime love, I'm sure you weren't thinking, *You know, I bet I can ruin our life and mess up this marriage within the next two months.*

Yet I read an article the other day about a new and disturbing trend in our culture. It's called trial marriages. It's for people who like the idea of being married, but are fearful of the commitment it entails, so they opt for a "practice" marriage. If things don't work out, that's okay . . . it just shows it wasn't meant to be to begin with. In order to protect themselves from a feeling of failure, they introduce the option of divorce at the very beginning. These couples agree not to share investments, assets, or children. After all, it's only practice for the real thing later on. The problem is, God designed human beings to commit in marriage to each other for a lifetime (Matthew 19:4-6). Anything less and your marriage will fall short of what God intended it to be.

ENEMIES OF SOULMATING

All marriages have specific enemies, from cultural pressures to workplace temptations. My friend Dr. Todd Linaman created a list of Marital Vulnerability Factors and wrote an article, "Are You Vulnerable for an Affair?" Take a few moments right now to carefully consider this list as you evaluate the state of your marriage:

- Unresolved anger toward your spouse that is easily triggered
- An unwillingness or inability to confront and resolve conflict

- An unmet hunger for intimacy and communication
- A belief that your spouse is to blame for your unhappiness
- A growing disinterest in spiritual matters and disciplines
- Increased isolation from friends and family
- Fantasizing about a life without your spouse
- A belief that your spouse will never change or be able to meet your needs
- Finding yourself easily and often attracted to the opposite sex
- Extended periods of high stress
- A general and pervasive feeling of dissatisfaction, discontentment, and boredom
- A growing feeling of indifference toward your spouse and marriage
- An increase in time spent away from your spouse and family
- Prolonged feelings of inadequacy, emptiness, and loneliness
- A growing pattern of deceit and deception
- Taking on a passive role in the marriage
- A belief that an affair could never happen to you[10]

Each of the above has the potential to undermine the SoulMating process in your marriage. I strongly encourage you to work on any of these factors that you believe are starting to creep into the heart of your marriage.

All marriages have enemies—an array of forces that aim to destroy whatever is intimate and good. By guarding against them and working to defuse them in your marriage, you can defeat these enemies and win the war for your marriage.

Just as there are enemies of SoulMating, there is a great Friend who designed your marriage to be a place where SoulMating can grow and flourish. And we know that this Friend is much more powerful than any enemy, as we read in 1 John 4:4 (NASB), "Greater is He who is in you than he who is in the world."

ENJOYING THE PROCESS

Starting out as a teenage couple, neither Donna nor I had a clue what love would require or what enemies would try to defeat us. We were just two kids getting married. I tell young people today that back then I was "hormone happy and brain-dead." We married as virgins, knew little about love, and nothing about being soul mates. We just knew we had made a commitment to each other—and that was enough.

Our marriage could easily have failed. Teenage marriages often don't ride the waves of marital reality very well. Without the loving support of family and the love of God, we could have become another statistic. But with thirty-plus years behind us now, I'm starting to understand a few things about what makes a marriage work. And I can tell you this: At age nineteen I couldn't have imagined ever being able to love Donna more than I did on our wedding night. But I do. In fact, I told her just last night, "Donna, it doesn't seem possible that I love you more today than I did yesterday, and I can't imagine that I will love you any more tomorrow, but I know I will."

In fact, here's my idea of a perfect day. Donna and I are alone in the car traveling down a highway, any highway, on a long road trip. There's no cell phone, no traffic delays, no deadlines, no mail, no schedule, and no children—just the two of us together riding, talking, and enjoying each other. We're free to stop the car when we want, speak whatever is on our mind without interruption, and talk about the kids—if we choose to. If you're a parent, you understand where I'm coming from. We just don't get enough days like that. I'd sum up the perfect day with the word *companionship*. I feel close to Donna when we spend time together sharing.

After many years of marriage, the SoulMating process continues in our relationship. SoulMating couples never arrive; they just keep on growing along the journey.

ENDNOTES

1 Henri Nouwen, *Christian Reader* (November/December 1996): 43-44. This quote originally appeared in *New Man* magazine.

2 Kevin Leman and Randy Carlson, *Unlocking the Secrets of Your Childhood Memories* (Nashville: Thomas Nelson, Inc., 1989), 148.

3 Erich Fromm, *The Art of Loving* (New York: Perennial Classics, 2000), 95.

4 Ted W. Engstrom, *The Fine Art of Friendship* (Nashville: Thomas Nelson, Inc., 1985). Found in Robert J. Morgan, *Nelson's Annual Preacher's Sourcebook* (Nashville: Thomas Nelson, 2001), 108.

5 "Reality Respect" is the author's marital adaptation of the work of Dr. Rudolf Dreikurs, *Children the Challenge* (New York: Hawthorn/Dutton, 1964) and the work of Dr. Alfred Adler. Many counseling professionals have built upon their excellent research, including Dr. Kevin Leman's work on "Reality Discipline."

6 Willard F. Harley Jr., *His Needs, Her Needs: Building an Affair-Proof Marriage* (Grand Rapids: Fleming H. Revell, 2001), 36.

7 Tim LaHaye and Beverly LaHaye and Mike Yorkey, *The Act of Marriage after 40* (Grand Rapids: Zondervan, 2000), 21.

8 Ibid., 32.

9 This list of rules has been circulated on the Internet in various adapted forms. The original "Ten Rules for a Happy Marriage" is attributed to an unnamed couple celebrating their fiftieth wedding anniversary who sent the list to Dear Abby.

10 Todd E. Linaman, "Are You Vulnerable for an Affair?" http://www.flc.org/hfl/marriage/mar-flm03.htm.

Other marriage resources available from Tyndale House Publishers

**The Married Guy's Guide
to Great Sex**
Clifford and Joyce Penner
ISBN 1-58997-153-1

Noted sex therapists Clifford and Joyce Penner describe what makes sex meaningful to a woman, while giving men great counsel on how to build desire, get past sexual problems, and discover what brings both partners incredible pleasure and intimacy. This candid, guilt-free book will help husbands get closer to their wives and get the love they want.

**20 (Surprisingly Simple)
Rules and Tools for a Great Marriage**
Dr. Steve Stephens
ISBN 0-8423-6203-7

Making simple changes can produce big positive results in your marriage. With clear, to-the-point principles, Dr. Stephens provides practical ways to keep your marriage strong and vibrant. Each chapter includes a prayer for strengthening your marriage and concrete ideas for helping you and your spouse enjoy each other as never before.

THE BOOK CLUB FOR TODAY'S CHRISTIAN FAMILY

A Letter to Our Readers

Dear Reader:

In order that we might better contribute to your reading enjoyment, we would appreciate your taking a few minutes to respond to the following questions. When completed, please return to the following:

Andrea Doering, Editor-in-Chief
Crossings Book Club
401 Franklin Avenue, Garden City, NY 11530

You can post your review online! Go to www.crossings.com and rate this book.

Title _____ Author _____

1   Did you enjoy reading this book?

❑ Very much. I would like to see more books by this author!

❑ I really liked_____

❑ Moderately. I would have enjoyed it more if_____

2   What influenced your decision to purchase this book? Check all that apply.

        ❑ Cover
        ❑ Title
        ❑ Publicity
        ❑ Catalog description
        ❑ Friends
        ❑ Enjoyed other books by this author
        ❑ Other _____

3   Please check your age range:

        ❑ Under 18   ❑ 18-24
        ❑ 25-34   ❑ 35-45
        ❑ 46-55   ❑ Over 55

4   How many hours per week do you read? _____

5   How would you rate this book, on a scale from 1 (poor) to 5 (superior)?
_____

Name_____

Occupation_____

Address_____

City_____ State_____ Zip_____